The Charles L. Allen Treasury

Books by CHARLES L. ALLEN

ROADS TO RADIANT LIVING
IN QUEST OF GOD'S POWER
GOD'S PSYCHIATRY
WHEN THE HEART IS HUNGRY
THE TOUCH OF THE MASTER'S HAND
ALL THINGS ARE POSSIBLE THROUGH PRAYER
WHEN YOU LOSE A LOVED ONE
THE TWENTY-THIRD PSALM
TWELVE WAYS TO SOLVE YOUR PROBLEM
HEALING WORDS
THE LIFE OF CHRIST
THE LORD'S PRAYER
PRAYER CHANGES THINGS
THE TEN COMMANDMENTS
THE SERMON ON THE MOUNT
THE BEATITUDES
LIFE MORE ABUNDANT
THE CHARLES L. ALLEN TREASURY

The

Charles L. Allen

Treasury

EDITED BY

Charles L. Wallis

FLEMING H. REVELL COMPANY
OLD TAPPAN, NEW JERSEY

SBN 8007-0398-7

Contents

Foreword

1 Meet the Master 9
2 The Timeless Appeal of Christ 25
3 My God, How Great Thou Art 37
4 Your Life Should Be Full 53
5 Hallmarks of Christian Living 71
6 Here's a Faith for You 93
7 Walk Through the Portals of Prayer 105
8 Christ Offers You Salvation 121
9 Decisions Disciples Make 135
10 I Love Thy Kingdom, Lord 151
11 Healing for the Troubled 163
12 Look Forward Hopefully 179
Index 189

Foreword

Ordinary guidelines for measuring spiritual leadership seem inadequate when appraising the distinctiveness of Dr. Charles L. Allen in contemporary Christian life. His remarkable pulpit ministry, the worldwide circulation of his books, and the stimulating and contagious appeal of his heart and mind say something concerning Dr. Allen, but they fall short of a full explanation.

In his written and spoken words and in the warmth of his personality may be found the key to his considerable influence. He writes with lucidity and in a transparently genuine way. His relevant and applicable ideas translate the timeless Gospel of Christ into the idiom and according to the needs of our generation. His manner is devotional and salubrious. His focus is on the individual reader. His picture-making power gives luster to his words, and his words radiate a faith that is vital and victorious.

This book is a golden harvest reaped from the pages of Dr. Allen's books. Here in both brief and extended quotation he shows how we can live creatively and courageously and with conviction and consecration.

This is not a bookish book. Rather, these pages mirror a life lived among people and echo the sounds of the street, the counselling room, the parish, the sports arena and the open fields. Above all, these pages interpret Dr. Allen's deep flowing love of Christ and his love and concern for people with whom he has found an unusual empathy.

CHARLES L. WALLIS

1

Meet The Master

So often we talk about the second coming of Christ as if He is helpless until then. My dear friends, Christ is here now. That is what makes the Christian faith so different from every other religion. Our Lord is not One who merely once lived and told us how to live. He lives now. The Christian shrine is not at a grave in some garden. That grave is empty—deserted.

MEET THE MASTER

He was born in a village, of poor parents in an insignificant little country. When He was twelve years old He was conscious of the fact that God had placed Him here for a specific purpose. At the age of thirty He made public His plans and purposes and began the three short years of His public ministry.

He loved people and enjoyed being with them. He went to their parties; He was a popular dinner guest; even the little children crowded around Him. He invited twelve men to work with Him, and later He commissioned them to carry on His work. He told a ruler about an experience called the "new birth."

He offered an outcast woman water that would quench the thirst of her very soul. He healed the sick, raised the dead, opened the eyes of the blind, loosed the tongues of the dumb, brought hearing to the deaf, and caused the lame to walk. He fed those who were hungry, and brought peace to troubled minds.

He taught the people that happiness comes from the inside, that the solution to hates and prejudices is not in laws but in love. He told of the amazing power of prayer, that the treasures one lays up in heaven are more important than the treasures one accumulates on earth, that a divided heart leads to destruction.

Faith in God was to Him a matter of supreme importance. Because God so beautifully clothed the lilies of the field, and because God cared so tenderly for even the birds of the air, He concluded that humans who are to live eternally should not worry about the things of this life. Instead, one should seek God's kingdom first and the other things of life would be taken care of.

He warned against people judging each other. He warned that a life built on any other principles than the ones He taught would be like a house built on sand that would not stand in the face of a storm.

He said that His Kingdom was like the growth of the tiny seed that eventually becomes a tree, or like the leaven that eventually leavens the entire loaf. And that possessing Him was worth all else one had, just as the merchant sold all his possessions in order to own the one pearl of supreme worth.

When one of His disciples suggested, after a marvelous worship experience, that He just continue there, He refused. Every mountain-top experience of worship was translated by Him into acts of service and of living. He said that the way to become great was to become a servant.

Firmly He taught that one is never justified in holding an unforgiving spirit. To a crowd which was preparing to stone a sinner to death He suggested that the one without sin cast the first stone. And to the sinner He said, "Neither do I condemn thee, go and sin no more." He loved sinners and freely forgave everyone who would accept forgiveness.

Simple stories from every day life illustrated the eternal principles He taught. The Samaritan who turned aside to help one in need, the foolish rich man who thought of his physical needs but forgot his soul, the shepherd who hunted until he found just one lost sheep, the father who welcomed his prodigal son home, are some of those stories.

He wept with friends who had lost a loved one by death. He was disappointed when some people He had healed expressed no gratitude. He pointed out that God expects every person to do his part, even though he has only one talent.

He cursed a fig tree for not producing fruit. He drove people out of the church who were misusing it. He said that we have duties to our government and duties to God. He praised a widow who gave a small gift.

He did not want to die, but He chose death rather than lower His standards. But as He died He prayed for the forgiveness of those who were killing Him, He gave comfort to a man dying with Him, He thought of the care of His mother, and He expressed His faith in God.

Three days after He was buried, He came back to life. He spoke to a woman, He encouraged some disheartened people, He spoke peace to His disciples, and one morning He even cooked their breakfast. He told His few followers to carry on His work until it covers the world, and finally He ascended into heaven.

He is today the one hope of the world. He is Jesus Christ, the Son of God and the Saviour of man.

IMAGE OF GOD

Man sees a little of God in many forms, majesty in His mountains, greatness in His seas, loveliness in His flowers, righteousness in His saints. But all of these are insufficient. With Philip, the heart of each of us says, "Lord, show us the Father." Jesus replied, "He that hath seen me hath seen the Father" (JOHN 14:8,9). The only perfect image of God we have is Christ, and that is sufficient.

As you see Him through the words of the Gospels—Matthew, Mark, Luke, and John, you are impressed with His eyes. Those who were with Him in the flesh neglected to tell us much about His physical appearance, but they could not forget His eyes. "And the Lord turned, and looked upon Peter" (LUKE 22:61), and Peter broke down. Sometimes Jesus' eyes flashed with merriment, sometimes they melted in tenderness, and other times they were filled with stern rebuke. When I read, "The ways of man are before the eyes of the Lord" (PROVERBS 5:21), I stop still in my tracks and think on my ways.

When we look at Jesus' face we know it was a happy face. Little children ran to get in His lap and clasp Him around His neck. People invited Him to their parties. Seeing God in Christ, we are not afraid of Him; instead we want to be closer to Him. We listen as He says, "Neither do I condemn thee; go and sin no more" (JOHN 8:11), and we are ashamed of our sins, we want forgiveness, and we come to Him repenting and asking for His cleansing.

We look as "he steadfastly set his face to go to Jerusalem" (LUKE 9:51). Though it meant death, He would not go back on the high purposes of His life. Seeing Him puts the steel in our own backbones to make the right decision. We watch as He walked seven miles to Emmaus to give hope to the downhearted (LUKE 24:13-32), or as He gave a new chance to His friends who failed Him (JOHN 20:19-31), and we take new heart and new hope.

HIS MAGIC POWER

One day the most magnificent Personality who has ever walked on this earth said to a group of very simple and ordinary people, "Come ye after me and I will make you. . ." (MARK 1:17). As He walked with them He exuded some kind of a strange influence over their lives.

Today our choirs sing the majestic *Te Deum* that tells about "the glorious company of the apostles." And who is that glorious company? Why it is wishy-washy Simon Peter, hot-headed John, doubting Thomas, calculating Matthew, fisherman James, and the others. But He "made them."

I know of no surer way of becoming a magnificent person than by getting intimately acquainted with Jesus Christ and letting His magic power work in you.

THE WAY OF CHRIST

Some people are so busy explaining things that they do not have time to do much. I doubt if Jesus attended many forums or discussion groups. He was so busy changing people and situations that He had little time for idle talk and speculations.

He might have preached lengthy sermons on the dignity of labor, temptation, how to enjoy life, the immortality of the soul, the worth of children, and the fact that God answers prayer. Instead, He worked in a carpenter's shop, He met and conquered temptation in the wilderness, He went to parties and laughed with other happy people, He raised the dead, He stopped His sermon to love little children, and after He prayed "the power of the Lord was present."

He might have talked long and loud about the need of man for human sympathy, the worth of womanhood, the blessing of humility, and the equal worth of all men. Instead, He wept at the grave of a friend, He treated all women with deep respect, He took a towel and washed His disciples' feet, He gave His time to the poor and outcasts.

Instead of talking about how He could transform lives, He took a harlot and made her the first herald of His resurrection. Instead of arguing that spirit is stronger than matter, He walked on the water. Instead of preaching that people need bread, He fed the multitude. Instead of telling how bad it is to be crippled, He said, "Arise, take up thy bed, and walk" (MARK 2:9). Instead of merely telling people they should forgive, while He was dying and being spit upon He prayed, "Father, forgive them" (LUKE 23:34). Instead of theorizing about God, He said, "I am the way" (JOHN 14:6).

To aid my memory, I have developed the habit of writing notes to myself. On my desk I always keep a note pad on which I scribble notes, such as, visit So and So, write such and such a letter, attend that meeting, and so on. And long ago I found that I needed aids to prompt my memory about even the supreme things of life. On the walls of my study are pictures that remind me of Christ. In my home are pictures of Him. Where I live and work I want something that will not let me forget the biggest thing in my life—my relationship to God.

JESUS, TOO, HAD TO WAIT

Christ said, ". . . I must be about my Father's business . . ." (LUKE 2:49); "I came . . . not to do mine own will, but the will of him that sent me" (JOHN 6:38); ". . . he that hath sent me is with me" (JOHN 8:29).

As some poet has said

> Jesus, too, had a Promised Land,
> But it wasn't a place,
> It was a plan.

A plan for His life, a work to be done, a place to be filled; God's plan for Christ was the establishment of a kingdom—the Kingdom of God. It meant the creating on earth of a society in which love, peace, and righteousness would reign. It was a thrilling and glorious way to spend one's life.

Yet Jesus, too, had to wait in some land of bondage. His Egypt was a carpenter's shop. Circumstance was the pharaoh that held Him in captivity. No doubt Joseph had died when Jesus was a teen-age boy. On His shoulders fell the responsibility of earning a living for Himself and

Mary and his smaller brothers and sisters. No doubt His ambition was to go to college, but He forever lost that chance. Circumstances stood in the way of His dreams and brought disappointment instead of fulfillment.

Jesus had to wait, and wait, and wait to get out of bondage and to journey toward His promised land. But maybe the waiting was part of God's plan for His Son.

Within the breast of Christ was burning a fire. It was the consciousness of God's plan for His life. Surely He was anxious to get started, to see results, to achieve His life's purpose. But circumstances held Him in slavery.

Instead of preaching the good news of the Kingdom, He was forced to saw planks and hammer nails. It was such menial work for the Son of God to be doing. It caused Him to miss going to college. Every day He was held back, it seemed, was a day lost. But the days went into months and into years, and still He had to wait. His chance did not come until He was thirty years old. In those days, thirty years old was approaching old age.

But as you study His entire life, you begin to feel that the waiting was part of God's plan. Certainly Jesus used His circumstances in the finest possible way. Instead of becoming bitter, instead of surrendering His dreams, instead of turning to some lesser purpose, He held fast to His promised land and at the same time was faithful to life, day by day. As we study His later ministry, we see that the opportunities of His limited "today" became the stones out of which He built His castle tomorrow.

He became trained and conditioned in the school of experience, instead of in college. I don't know what the scholars might have taught Him, but we do know many of the things He learned day by day, and we know how He used His knowledge for the glory of God.

Someone imagines that one day a farmer came to him for estimates on the building of a new barn. While at Jesus' shop, the farmer boasted loudly of his great abundance and talked profanely about the kind of life he lived. But the next week that farmer's son came to Jesus to get a coffin made in which to bury his father. As Jesus made the coffin, He thought about that man and the mistakes he had made. Later Jesus was not in the carpenter's shop; instead He was preaching to the multitudes. He saw in them a mad desire for things. He remembered that farmer of past years, and He told them the story (LUKE 12:16-21). It was a story they could understand, and by the use of that experience, Jesus taught the truth of God.

So it was with all of those matchless stories He told. They came out of life, His own life, and they had great meaning for the people. In the school of experience Jesus learned well the lessons of life, and as a result, the Bible says, ". . . the common people heard him gladly" (MARK 12:37). Being able to win the common people, helped Him gain the followers who would carry on His work.

WALKING WITH CHRIST

One should think of making his entire life a walk with Christ. To accomplish that, however, one must learn to walk four roads.

1. There is the Damascus Road—the road of conversion. Saul, whose name was later changed to Paul, was on his way to Damascus. He had recently seen Stephen die for his faith in Christ and doubtless he realized that Stephen had found something that he, Saul, had missed. As he journeyed along, he suddenly felt the spirit of Christ. Christ said to him, "Why persecutest thou me?" Saul replied, "What wilt thou have me to do?" (ACTS 9:1-6). From then on, his life was determined by the will of Christ.

To others, the experience of conversion might not come in a dramatic fashion. It might be a growing experience of the presence of Christ, as the years have come and gone. How and when it comes is not most important, but rather the reality of the knowledge of His saving power is the important thing. To walk with Christ, one must reach the point of commitment to Christ's will.

2. We must learn to walk the Jericho Road—the road of service. On that road there lay a man who was wounded and needed help. Some came that way but passed by on the other side. One man stopped and helped. Speaking of the one who helped, Jesus said, "Go, and do thou likewise" (LUKE 10:30-37).

Some people walk the road of self-interest. They are opposed to any sort of foreign aid, they refuse to give to the Community Chest, the Red Cross and many other causes. They complain about "too many collections." Such people have no sense of obligation toward their fellow man. But Christ is not found on that road. To walk with Him, we must remember His words: "I am among you as he that serveth" (LUKE 22:27). In order to walk with Christ, one must surrender his selfishness.

3. There is the road to Calvary—the road of suffering. Christ could have escaped this road but had He done so, He would not have been the Saviour. Suffering is part of the portion of living and in order to walk with Christ, we must not only bear the sorrow, we must so use our sorrow as to make it a blessing.

A young mother saw her little daughter suffer a severe fall and die a few days later. The mother's world went to pieces. She secluded herself in anguish and despair. Then one day the voice of God seemed to say to her, "Have you ever thought of the many girls who have no mother and need one? Why don't you use your love for them?" Her name was Josephine Webb, and she rendered magnificent service from then on. She learned to walk the road of suffering with Christ.

4. There is the Emmaus Road—the road of fellowship. As two disciples walked together one day, the Lord joined in step with them. They later recognized Him as He broke bread in their home. As a result of that experience, they learned that Christ was on every road they walked; He was in their home, He was with them whatever they were doing. They realized His daily presence, His wonderful power and love.

When we come to Him through faith, He always does for us that which most needs to be done. Sometimes He lifts the burden; at other times He gives us added strength to bear the burden. Sometimes He changes the circumstances of our lives; at other times He gives us the wisdom to use those circumstances for our own good. Sometimes He makes different the situation which we face; at other times He makes different the person in the situation.

GOD'S PURGING

Modern congregations have about discarded the old mourners' bench. It was a place where penitents came seeking divine pardon. In its stead we have a psychological clinic. Certainly I do not disparage the help of modern psychology. I have spent untold hours in counseling, but counseling by itself is not enough.

Today we want God's blessings without the pain of God's purging. We want sermons on how to win friends, how to have peace of mind, and how to forget our fears. But we must remember that Christ came to make men good rather than merely to make men feel good.

Each Sunday night in my own church I give people a chance to come and pray at the altar. Watching tears streaming down some praying face, I have felt like shouting for joy. The way of the Cross is not easy, but it is the way home.

Jesus told us, "And I, if I be lifted up from the earth, will draw all men unto me." Then the Gospel record adds, "This he said, signifying what death he should die" (JOHN 12:32,33). And as we see the suffering of the Saviour, surely it must bring suffering to us. Only a dead soul can see Him without mourning.

Let us remember that it is the sins of men that put Him there. If men had traveled less the paths of sin, His path up Calvary would have been less steep. If they had been less greedy and self-seeking, the nails in His hands would have burned less. If they had been less proud, His crown of thorns would have been less painful. If they had loved others more, they would have hated Him less.

On the cross He said, "Father, forgive them; for they know not what they do" (LUKE 23:34). Surely Pilate and Caiphas, Herod and the soldiers did not know what they were doing. Greedy, selfish men were merely putting out of the way one who got in their way. Their very ignorance helped Him to bear His cross.

But we do know. We have the record which has been taught to us from childhood. We are the ones who grieve him most, who make the pain for Him the hardest to bear. He died to heal our broken hearts, and, instead, we break His heart by our own sin and our indifference to Him.

PROOF OF GOD'S LOVE

Jesus was born nearly two thousand years ago, was crucified at about the age of thirty-three, and was buried. In three days He was up and living again, visiting and talking with His friends for a few weeks. Then He left them, and no one has seen His physical body since.

Since that happened, men have sought to understand the true meaning of it all. Great numbers have believed that Jesus was God—that the great

God who made the earth came and walked on it for a time, and in doing so left a true picture of Himself.

The record of Jesus' life on earth is the only real proof of God's love and compassion. You cannot find such a picture of God in nature. True, there are beautiful flowers, majestic mountain peaks, and gentle rains from heaven. But there are also fierce storms, the withering heat of the sun, and the dread disease of cancer.

But we can understand this God who came to earth "to seek and to save that which was lost" (LUKE 19:10). He came on a mission, and to accomplish it He gave Himself as a ransom for the sins and shortcomings of mankind. The cross will forever stand as our supreme evidence of a loving, suffering, forgiving God.

COURAGE NEEDED

"If thou be willing, remove this cup from me" (LUKE 22:42). The great temptation of life is to follow our own desires, to make our own plans, to be guided by our own wills—and to hope God is willing.

But suppose God is not willing? Then we have only one of two choices: to renounce God's will and follow our own, or to renounce our own will and follow God's. And most of the time we must make that choice without fully knowing what God's will is. That requires more faith than some people have. It requires more courage than some people have. It never is an easy decision to make. Jesus' struggle was so great that sweat like great drops of blood began to pour from His face to the ground.

The suffering of Jesus was a thousand times greater than that of the thieves on the crosses by His side. They experienced the same pain but not the same suffering.

Burdens and thorns are thrust upon us, but only volunteers carry crosses.

HIS STATUS SYMBOL

According to our standards of success, Jesus was one of the failures of history. He disappointed His friends and followers. His family considered Him a hopeless dreamer. He was trained for a respectable trade but turned His back upon it. He never drew a salary, never saved any money, never even owned a house in which to live. He achieved none of the status symbols that we consider so important—a flashy new car, two television sets, an honorary degree, and so on. The only status symbol He achieved was a cross on which He suffered a lonely death. What a tragedy for such a fine young Man to come to such a dreary end! Today we call Him "Lord," but multitudes of us do not really worship the kind of success that He achieved.

THE SEVEN WORDS

It is a stimulating and helpful experience to put before oneself the seven sentences of Christ on the Cross. So I am listing them in the order it is generally believed they were spoken by our Lord.

1. "Father forgive them, for they know not what they do" (LUKE 23:34). Jesus had very real grievances—the rulers had opposed Him and plotted His death, His disciples had betrayed Him, the people had chosen sorry Barabbas over Him, His trial had been unjust, He had been mocked, cursed and spit upon, His friends had deserted Him. But when He prays for the forgiveness of "them" He means all of them. There is no bitterness in His heart. In a beautiful act of charity, He even excuses them and seeks to remove their guilt by saying they do not know what they do. This is surely a time for each of us to throw the blanket of love and forgiveness over those who have done us wrong—to wipe the slate clean by extending our own forgiveness and seeking even for those who have wronged us the forgiveness of the Father.

2. "Today shalt thou be with me in paradise" (LUKE 23:43). It was the word of hope for a wasted and misspent life. It reveals the heart of the Eternal that is ever eager to reclaim and restore even the least and the

last and the lost. It is His word that this life is not the end but rather the entrance into a larger one.

3. "Woman, behold thy son. Son, behold thy mother" (JOHN 19:26). Even as He is suffering the agony of death He has a word of compassion and concern for one whom He loves. In the midst of more pain than it seems anyone could bear He still is anxious about the needs and well-being of another. Here is a rebuke to selfishness, a shame for hardheartedness. It reveals that we ourselves are living at our very best when we can turn away from our own sorrows and disappointments and seek to meet a need in a weaker life.

4. "My God, my God, why hast thou forsaken me?" (MARK 15:34). This is the only question He ever asked God, and I believe it to be a very real one. It is His human side that is so clearly revealed here in a momentary sense of forsakenness—an experience that we all have some time or another. Every person somewhere along the way of life feels that God has let him down. It is well to recall in such times that the resurrection followed the crucifixion. Victory is always the last word with God.

5. "I thirst" (JOHN 19:28). Here is represented the physical price that Christ paid—the cost of something grand and glorious. There are no short cuts to the things that really matter. And, also, it represents His very deep thirst for God just now. In the midst of suffering even He who was so close is drawn even closer to the Father. Not always is that so. A sorrow makes us either bitter or better. But for those who will see and feel, God is closer in times of deep sorrow than at any other time.

6. "It is finished" (JOHN 19:30). Better than any of us, I think, can the boys who were at the front when the armistice came understand all that is wrapped up in those words of our Lord. The blood of the battlefield, the agony of the strain of battle, the homesickness in a faraway land, and then—"It is finished"—the victory is won. That is what Christ felt, only on a much grander scale. His task was finished. His Kingdom was planted, and the "gates of hell shall not prevail against it."

7. "Father, into thy hands I commend my spirit" (LUKE 23:46). It was a cry of faith. He had done His best. He had given His all. Now He was willing to leave the results to God. And we, too, when we have done our best, need not worry or fear. God always takes care of the results. This was also a cry of refuge—even as we sing, "Jesus, Lover of my soul, let me to Thy bosom fly. . . . Safe into the haven guide; O receive my soul at last."

What great words to have before us throughout life—the seven sentences of Christ on the Cross.

Read the New Testament. Never one time does Jesus promise ease to His followers. As He called man to follow Him, Jesus did not talk about the golden streets and gates of pearl in the next life. Instead, He talked about self-denial, about taking up a cross—not a pretty little gold cross that might be worn as an ornament, but a rough, blood-stained, death-dealing cross.

Jesus took the cross of sin and made it the cure for sin; He took the hate of man and made it the revelation of God's love; He took the harshest word of man and made it God's tenderest utterance. Jesus did not merely bear the cross; He used it for the salvation of the world. He turned sorrow into a song, Calvary into Easter. He is our example.

GOD'S MORNING

The most vivid portrayal of the trial, crucifixion and resurrection of Christ that I have ever seen was on television one Sunday afternoon. Had I know what was coming, I think I would have turned to something else and not have let our two little children (aged four and six) see it, but after it started we decided to let them see it all the way through.

They see all the fighting, shooting, and killing in the wild West pictures, but that doesn't bother them; they know it isn't real. But this was Jesus! Since they were old enough to learn, they had been taught that Jesus was good and kind and that He loved everybody. They sing "Jesus loves me, this I know," and they have come to love Him.

They saw men whipping Him, and it broke their hearts. When He was nailed to the cross, they cried. They had heard about the cross, but it had never been so real to them before. They could hardly bear it. Then He was buried, and I have never seen two more confused and unhappy children.

I told them to keep on watching and see what happened. Then Easter morning came. There were the women on the way to the tomb, feeling just as our own little children felt. But the resurrection came. He rose out of the grave and walked in the garden.

And what a marvelous relief and joy showed on the faces of those two little children. That little four-year-old girl gleefully said, "Jesus is all right. He has 'arised.'" The fact that everything came out so well in the end was all they needed to know.

Easter can be an ever-recurring experience. Many people go through severe trials. We are hurt very deeply. We feel the bitter injustice of many things that come our way. Many become confused and resentful. A lot of people give up and quit on some Calvary's hill in their own lives.

If only we would just be patient and keep on doing the best we can under the circumstances, we would learn that Easter comes after Calvary. Read the story of the creation in the first chapter of Genesis. There we find it written: "And the evening and the morning were the first day."

God's day ends with the morning. There comes into almost every life a dark night, and it is so easy to feel that is the end, that it will always be dark. But on Easter we know that Calvary is never the final word. And through faith we know that after the dark comes the sunrise.

2

The Timeless Appeal of Christ

*The arm of Christ is no less
than twenty centuries long.*

WHY THEY SOUGHT HIM

Why were people so interested in Jesus? There are several reasons:
1. Once a leper came and when Jesus saw him He was "moved with compassion" (MARK 1:41). Throughout His ministry we find that He was concerned about the needs of people and He loved them. Never once did He turn His back on any person who came to Him seeking help. When He spoke, people knew He was trying to help them. We are interested in the preacher who is interested in us. As people heard Him they realized: Here is one who is different; He is not trying to get something out of me; He is offering something to me.
2. Crowds came to hear Jesus because He had something important to say. After He had finished the Sermon on the Mount, the Bible tells us the people were astonished at Him "for he taught them as one having authority" (MATTHEW 7:29). Jesus had the answers for the problems of man and He still has them. Thus we are anxious to hear what He says.
3. Crowds came to Jesus because He spoke in a language the people could understand. Mark tells us, "The common people heard him gladly" (MARK 12:37). Jesus never tried to impress people with big words, but rather did He express the truth of God so that even the most unlearned would be helped.
4. Crowds came to hear Christ because no one else could offer what He did. Once He asked His disciples, "Will ye also go away?" Peter replied, "Lord, to whom shall we go?" (JOHN 6:67, 68). And that answer still holds. Where is there another who offers to us and to our world what Christ offers? If we should turn our backs on Him, where would we go?

WHY CHRIST UNDERSTANDS

The one thing I have to offer people is a Christ who knows what a hard time is. We have made Him a Christ of stained-glass windows, of sweet sentiments and fine hymns. But in the days of His flesh, he was the Christ of life that was hard and disappointing. Certainly He understands any person who is having a hard time.

Look at the home in which He lived. In one of His stories He tells about how the candle lighted the whole house. He was probably talking from personal experience, describing the house He had lived in. If one candle would light the house it had to be only one room.

Being the oldest of eight children, Jesus had to drop out of school when His father died in order to make a living for the others. Jesus was thirty before He could get started in His life's work.

He talks about clothes that were patched and then repatched. That is, the patches were patched. When He talks about food, it is usually fish and bread, the food of the poor. Jesus personally knew very few of the luxuries of life. He knew what it was to have a hard time.

However, His life is a shining example of the words of St. Paul, "All things work together for good to them that love God" (ROMANS 8:28).

Because of His own poverty He could preach to the common people, and they heard Him gladly. He stood on the same level with people who needed help and because He could help them, He won them, and later these same common people spread His name over all the earth.

Early in life He learned about children, and when His disciples were turning children away, Jesus said, "Suffer little children . . . to come unto me" (MATTHEW 19:14). And through the stream of Christianity, mercy and love for little children have flowed. Our little children sing with assurance, "Jesus loves me, this I know."

The difficulties of that small, congested home prepared Him for His place as head of the family of God. When He saw His disciples—older children—fussing and complaining, He did not lose faith in them. He knew that even children of the same family have their little quarrels. Today He understands why we have so many different denominations, and I am sure He is not too displeased with His children fussing a little among themselves from time to time.

When He was a boy He worked with His father, but His father died, and as a young man Jesus must have missed His father terribly. But as He thought of His own father and as He thought of God, a truth of tremendous import burst upon Him. God is a father! Jesus was the first to teach us that.

At the age of only thirty-three He faced His death. He was so young to die. There was so much He wanted to do. But even on the cross He still kept his faith. He turned His face upward and said, "Father, into thy hands I commend my spirit" (LUKE 23:46).

Even the cross worked out for good. Today it is embedded in the hearts of millions, and it is slowly redeeming the world.

I like to work with a Christ like Him.

How Jesus comes is incidental. He may come walking across the water, or through the inspiration of a church service, or through the help of some friend, or through some change in the circumstances of your life, or in one of many ways. The important thing is that when we feel the need of Him and are ready to receive Him, He knows it and always comes.

TESTIMONY OF HIS CRITICS

Let us recall that it was from the critics of Jesus that He received some of His greatest compliments. Often you can judge a man better by what his enemies say about him than by what his friends say; so let me call the enemies of Christ to the witness stand and hear their testimony.

Number one: "Never man spake like this man" (JOHN 7:46). These were the words of the officers who were sent to arrest Him. He gave to the world a new language, a language of hope which pointed to a better way.

The religious language of that day was full of prohibitions. There were countless laws, and over and over the people were told that they would be cursed and punished for breaking those laws. St. Mark tells us: "Jesus came into Galilee, preaching the gospel [good news] of the kingdom of God" (1:14). Eighty-eight times He told people how they could be "blessed." His words were not to condemn, but to help, and He put them so simply and winsomely that even "the common people heard him gladly" (MARK 12:37).

Number two: ". . . behold, the world is gone after him" (JOHN 12:19). This was the testimony of jealous Pharisees. They were saying that when people came to know Him, they followed Him. The authorities killed Him, but the world is still going after Him. Wesley sang,

O, for a thousand tongues to sing,
My great redeemer's praise.

Today His praise is being sung in more than a thousand tongues; in fact, in two hundred more than a thousand tongues: His words are now translated into 1,200 languages and dialects.

Number three: "Is not this the carpenter . . . ?" (MARK 6:3). These words were said sneeringly by people of His home town. They were right. The carpenter can take rough-hewn timbers and make of them a castle. Jesus is taking men and women who are sinners, redeeming and refining them, and using them to build "colonies of heaven." He is fashioning men and women into likenesses of Himself, and with them He is building the Kingdom of God on earth.

Number four: "He saved others; himself he cannot save" (MATTHEW 27:42). This was said by those who were seeking to mock Him, but they were only mocking themselves. To become a Saviour of the suffering, He had to become a suffering Saviour. Poor, blind, selfish men! They are the ones who were not saved. They refused to listen when He told them: "He that findeth his life shall lose it: and he that loseth his life for my sake shall find it" (MATTHEW 10:39). We can never save ourselves except by giving ourselves to something greater than ourselves. In the saving of others, we do save ourselves.

Number five: "Then said the Jews, Behold how he loved him?" (JOHN 11:36). This was spoken by His criticis as they watched Him weeping at the grave of Lazarus. And not only Lazarus did He love; He loved the young ruler, the sinful woman, the poor beggar at the gate. Not only did He love John, who loved Him; also He loved Judas, who betrayed Him. Not only did He love the little children, who rushed into His arms; also He loved those who nailed Him to the cross. And, best of all, He loves me. So we sing, "O, Love, that wilt not let me go."

Number six: "This is Jesus the king of the Jews" (MATTHEW 27:37). They nailed those words above His head, but almost two thousand years later multitudes of people stand and sing, "King of kings, forever and ever." No other king has commanded even a fraction of the following He commands today. He is *The King.*

Number seven: ". . . he made himself the Son of God" (JOHN 19:7). This was a charge hurled against Him at His trial. Today, millions are still saying it. Someone has said: "All the armies that ever marched, all the navies that were ever built, all the parliaments that have ever sat, and all the kings that have ever ruled, put together, have not affected the life of man upon this earth like this one solitary personality." What is the explanation? Napoleon said, "I know men, and I know Jesus Christ was no man." He was truly God.

In one of the European galleries there is a very fine statue of Apollo, a beautiful example of physical perfection. They say it is interesting to watch the crowds pass by that statue. When a person sees it, he invariably begins to straighten up. He isn't conscious of what he is doing, but seeing that statue, he wants to be like it.

That is the motive of the Christian: he sees Christ and in Christ he sees life. Seeing that, he instinctively wants to move toward it. Then it is no sacrifice to turn loose whatever may hinder him and to walk the "strait and narrow path."

Jesus' call is to every man—maybe not to leave his work, but certainly to leave his sin; maybe not to be a full-time disciple, but certainly to be a full-time Christian.

FRIEND OF SINNERS

One of the most beloved chapters of the Bible is Luke 15. I like the way it begins: "Then drew near unto Him, all the publicans and sinners, for to hear Him." That tells us a lot about Christ. It means that those who had failed, realized that in Him they would find help instead of condemnation. We are told that He was "a friend of sinners," that He liked to eat with them, that He gave most of His time to them. He had harsh words for self-righteous people, but always He spoke kindly to those who had missed the way. In fact, the word "sinner" was seldom on His lips. He thought of them as "lost."

PRIORITIES

Following Jesus means that He must be put first. He demands that love for Him must take precedence above even the love we have for our own families—our fathers or mothers, our sons or daughters; there can be no rivals to our affection for Him. "He that loveth father or mother more than me is not worthy of me: and he that loveth son or daughter more than me is not worthy of me" (MATTHEW 10:37).

It is very popular today to say that religion can make one successful, happy, confident, and relaxed. But Jesus doesn't appeal to the selfish desires of those who would follow Him. Instead, following Him demands a cross. His words were: ". . . he that taketh not his cross, and followeth after me, is not worthy of me" (MATTHEW 10:38).

If Jesus lived today in the flesh, rode in jet airplanes, watched television, lived in an air-conditioned home, had all the information which scientists have gained in reference to outer space, and had access to all of today's scientific knowledge, He still would not need to change one word of the Sermon on the Mount. The words which he spoke are eternal and apply equally to every age and to every generation. In fact, He Himself felt that His words were even more enduring than this universe. He said, "Heaven and earth shall pass away: but my words shall not pass away" (MARK 13:31).

NO MORE MIRACLES?

Walk down the street and ask the people you meet, "Do you believe Christ actually performed miracles?" The overwhelming majority will say, "Yes." Most of us do not question that fact that He made the crippled walk, the blind see, the sick well. We accept without hesitation the fact that the winds and the waves obeyed His voice.

Ask those same people, "Do you believe Christ can and will work those same miracles today?" Usually you will get a stammering reply of double-talk. Rarely will you get a clearcut answer of "Yes." Most people to not believe that Christ will work a miracle in their very own lives.

Ask the same people, "If Christ were here today in the flesh, do you believe He could and would work the miracles like unto those when He was in Galilee?" Again, most people would immediately say, "Yes." The conclusion is clear: most people today really feel that the physical presence of Christ is necessary to the expression of His power.

OBEDIENCE REQUIRED

Why is it many people fail to experience His miracle-working power? It is because they do not meet the one requirement. As the condition of His help, He requires from us faith which leads to obedience. His mother said to the servants at the wedding, "Whatsoever he saith unto you, do it." If they had not had faith enough to do what they were told, the miracle never would have been performed.

Before Christ fed the multitude, a little boy gave Him his lunch. Before the sick woman was healed, she touched the hem of His garment. Before the lame man was healed, four men brought him to Jesus. Before the blind man could see, he obeyed the command of Christ to go wash in the pool. Before Christ raised Lazarus from the dead, someone had to roll the stone away from his grave. Before the crippled man at the pool was made whole, he obeyed the Lord, stood and took up his bed.

Study our Lord's life. You will see He knew something about the everyday struggle to make ends meet. He knew the meaning of the widow's two mites, what a disaster the loss of a coin might be, wearing clothes which were patched. He knew about shopping in the grocery store to try to stretch a budget to feed the family. He talks about the housewife who must buy two birds which sold for a penny.

Even on the resurrection side of the grave our Lord was concerned with bread. We see Him walking home with two of His friends on that first Easter Sunday. He spoke hope to their hearts, and He also took time to sit at the table with them. In fact, the Bible says, "He took bread, and blessed it, and brake, and gave to them" (LUKE 24:30).

In the gray dawn of the morning we see Him on the seashore. His disciples had been fishing all night. Now they were coming in, and the Lord was prepared for them. What did He prepare? A prayer meeting? They needed prayer. A majestic and overwhelming revelation of Himself? They had lost faith in Him. No, He prepared breakfast.

The risen, resplendent Christ cooking breakfast! Though His feet were bruised, He walked over a rocky beach to gather firewood. Though His hands were nailpierced, He cleaned fish. He knew that the fishermen would be hungry.

He knows we have groceries to buy, rent or payments to make on our houses, clothes that are necessary, expenses for the children in school, bills of every sort to meet. Not only that, He knows we have desires and wants beyond our bare necessities. We are not wild beasts. We want some of the pleasant things of life.

Much better than we, He knew that the body and the soul are an inseparable unity. Just as worry and fear can affect the body and make one sick, so one's physical condition can affect a man's outlook on life, his religious faith, his moral conduct.

The God who made our bodies is concerned about the needs of our bodies, and He is anxious for us to talk with Him about our physical needs.

Every morning the sun rises to warm the earth. If it were to fail to shine for just one minute, all life on the earth would die. The rains come to water the earth. There is fertility in the soil, life in the seeds, oxygen in the air. The providence of God is about us in unbelievable abundance every moment. But so often we just take it for granted.

With infinite love and compassion our Lord understood the human predicament. He had deep empathy with people; He saw their needs, their weaknesses, their desires, and their hurts. He understood and was concerned for people. Every word He spoke was uttered because He saw a need for that word in some human life. His concern was always to uplift and never to tear down, to heal and never hurt, to save and not condemn.

FOCAL WINDOW

When I was a pastor in Atlanta, the church contracted with a firm in England for twenty-five stained-glass windows, presenting the life of

Christ. It was not too difficult to decide on the particular scenes to be used, except in one case.

Which scene from His life should be in the window back of the pulpit? Since that was the window the people would be looking into as they worshipped, we wanted to be sure it was the right one. What would it be? His birth? The Lord preaching, praying? The shepherd? The Last Supper? The cross? His resurrection? Any of those would have been appropriate, but we did not select any of them.

Just before His ascension, He said to His disciples, "Go ye . . . and, lo, I am with you alway . . ." (MATTHEW 28:19-20). This is the one we decided on for the focal point in the church. Think about it. These disciples had committed so many blunders and they were limited men in so many ways. They had even denied their Lord and had acted in a cowardly and shameful fashion. But in spite of that, Jesus was willing to trust His work into their hands and He promised His Presence and Power to them. Those men never faltered after that. When we believe ourselves to be within the will of God and know He is helping us, we will not fail.

3

My God How Great Thou Art!

It is so much easier to whittle God down to our size instead of repenting, changing our way of living, and being Godly ourselves.

THE GREATNESS OF GOD

Here is one of the grandest verses in the Bible: "When I consider thy heavens, the work of thy fingers, the moon and the stars, which thou hast ordained . . ." (PSALM 8:3).

Have you ever wondered why God made the world so beautiful, so impressive, so big? Nobody knows how big the heavens are with their millions, maybe billions, of stars. God didn't have to make it that big in order for the earth to exist. Why did God make it so that every morning the glory of a sunrise would come over the earth and every evening the quiet beauty of a sunset? He could have arranged it so the day would come and go in some less impressive manner.

Have you ever looked at a great mountain range and wondered why God made those high peaks? God could have left the mountains out of His creation. Mountains aren't really good for anything. They can't be cultivated; and beyond a certain point, they don't even grow trees. We do not need mountains in order to live on this earth.

I have flown across the trackless deserts of the West. As I looked at the endless miles of hot sand, I wondered why God made them that way. The deserts aren't good for anything. No food can grow there; the few creatures who live there are worthless to mankind.

Most impressed am I when I look at the ocean. Nobody really knows how big the ocean is. In places it is literally miles deep. It seems an awful waste. God could have fixed His creation so that rain could come without creating that vast reservoir of water. Why did He make the ocean?

God had a reason for making oceans, mountains, skies, and deserts. He never wastes anything. The Psalmist said, "When I consider thy heavens . . . ." The tragedy is that many people live amid God's creation and never consider it. A thoughtless person once said to Helen Keller, "Isn't it awful to be blind?" She replied, "Not half so bad as to have two good eyes and never see anything."

And there are people who are content with a mighty small world. They never "consider the heavens." They never really see anything big.

When you look into the face of the sky and consider something of its infinite size, you realize that no little God created it. He had to have big ideas and unlimited abilities. Truly we come to realize, "Our God is a great God." Realizing His greatness, we are not as afraid of what might happen in His world. Our troubles seem hard to bear, but nothing can defeat the will and purposes of the Eternal Father.

I have watched colossal storms roar across the mountains. Heavy clouds come thundering in and everything gets dark. You begin to wonder if the world isn't going to be destroyed. Then, the clouds break up and you see the green mountainside bathed in sunlight. And you know that if you wait out the storm, there will be sunlight again. When we have trouble and everything seems lost, with a picture of the greatness of God in mind, we gain courage and calmness.

On the other hand, when the sun is shining and the breezes are gentle, we know it will not always remain so. Sooner or later it will cloud up and rain again. So we make preparation during the good weather for the bad that is sure to follow. Likewise, when we are blessed with a life that is smooth and good, we remember that we must be ready for the trouble that is sure to come.

Realizing the greatness of God, our minds are stretched to take the long view of life, not living for just the moment but considering the whole.

We are in too big a hurry, and we run by far more than we catch up with. The Bible tells us to "be still, and know that I am God" (PSALM 46:10). Beauty doesn't shout. Loveliness is quiet. Our finest moods are not clamorous. The familiar appeals of the Divine are always in calm tones, a still, small voice. Here is the New Testament picture of Jesus: "Behold, I stand at the door, and knock: if any man hear my voice, and open the door, I will come in to him, and will sup with him, and he with me" (REVELATION 3:20). The Divine is not obtrusive. He bursts in no one's life unbidden. He is reserved and courteous.

ACQUAINTED WITH GOD

There are many ways to become better acquainted with God. The other day I was up in the mountains. Sitting there in the quiet coolness, my attention became fixed on a great mountain which I could see in the distance.

The peak of the mountain was obscured by a violent thunderstorm. The wind lashed it from every direction, the water poured down upon it in torrents, great bolts of lightning struck it heavy blows. I wondered if even a mountain could withstand such an onslaught. But after awhile the clouds were gone and there stood the mountain glistening in the bright sunlight.

I got to thinking about what that mountain had gone through. There had been many thunderstorms, earthquakes, and fires. It had known cold winters and the heavy burdens of ice and snow. During its lifetime the wars of the world had come and gone; depressions, kings had risen and fallen, civilizations had lived and died: but the mountain is still there. Looking at it I felt stronger and more secure.

A verse of Scripture came to mind: ". . . the strength of the hills is his also." Seeing that mountain, I became better acquainted with God. I turned to the Ninety-fifth Psalm, in which that verse is recorded, and I read the entire Psalm. It begins, "Oh come, let us sing unto the Lord: let us make a joyful noise." Why can we sing and be joyful? The psalmist tells us it is because of God. "For the Lord is a great God . . . the strength of the hills is his . . . The sea is his, and He made it . . ."; and triumphantly the psalmist declares, "For he is our God; and we are the people of his pasture. . . ."

UNSATISFIED HUNGERS

There is a vast multitude of people with unsatisfied hungers. Life is a hard, disappointing experience. They may live in gutters or in castles. It matters not how little or how much we have, if we fail to possess that which satisfies our deepest hungers. Many have become bitter and hopeless and find life not to be worth living. Some have been conquered by despair and have no heart and no reason to keep on trying.

In their search for satisfaction, some went off on the wrong trails. Now they see their wrongs, but upon their memories is stamped forever the shame of a miserable past. They would now like to do better but with the dirt on their souls, what is the use of trying? In youth there were dreams and stars to move toward, but the light of the stars had faded and the dreams serve only to mock and torment.

But though God is forgotten, He doesn't forget. God keeps putting unrest and dissatisfaction into that person's heart and one moment, suddenly he sees God. A God who can forgive sins, who can take the pieces of a broken life and put them back together again, who can give reason and purpose to living. The God who sent His Son not to condemn but to save. It is like finding buried treasure. Joyously we possess it, no matter what the cost, and a new life becomes ours. We become so happy.

HOW GOD REVEALS HIMSELF

There are three ways—maybe four—in which God reveals Himself. First, in His marvelous creation. "The heavens declare the glory of God; and the firmament showeth his handiwork" (PSALM 19:1). That is the first revelation God made of Himself. We stand at the seashore and are moved by the boundless expanse before us. When we remember that He can hold all the seas in "the hollow of his hand" (ISAIAH 40:12), then we see something of His power. Standing among great mountain peaks, His majesty is impressed upon us. Jesus stood reverently before a wild "lily of the field" and saw the glory of God (MATTHEW 6:28,29). "Earth's crammed with heaven, and every common bush afire with God," sings Mrs. Browning. We look into the heavens and see the infiniteness of God, and at a tiny snowflake and see His perfection. The sunset teaches us of His beauty.

Yet modern man is in danger of letting his own conceit blot out this revelation of God. Instead of praying for rain, we talk about making rain ourselves. We seed clouds, but who made the clouds? Jesus introduces us to a character much like ourselves. "The ground of a certain rich man brought forth plentifully; and he thought within himself, saying, What shall I do, because I have no room where to bestow my fruits? . . . I will pull down my barns, and build greater; and there will I bestow all my fruits and my goods" (LUKE 12;16,18). I—I—I; My—My—My. There is no sense of God. God is the creator he does not see.

Second, God reveals Himself through people. Through Moses we glimpse God's law, Amos showed us His justice, Hosea His love, and Micah His ethical standards. Someone was kind when we were sick, helped in time of trouble, was friendly when we were lonely. Someone we had wronged forgave in a spirit of love. In all such acts a little of God is revealed unto us. You better understand God because of the love of your mother, the consecrated life of some friend, the heroism of some Joan d'Arc. Corporate worship is so much more rewarding because we learn from each other.

God's supreme revelation of Himself is in Christ. "He that hath seen me hath seen the Father." As Harry Webb Farrington sang

> *I know not how that Bethlehem's Babe*
> *Could in the Godhead be.*
> *I only know the manger Child*
> *Has brought God's life to me.*
>
> *I know not how that Calvary's cross*
> *A world of sin could free.*
> *I only know its matchless love*
> *Has brought God's love to me*
>
> *I know not how that Joseph's tomb*
> *Could solve death's mystery;*
> *I only know a living Christ,*
> *Our immortality.*

As you read the four Gospels and see Jesus you begin to realize that you are actually seeing God.

One other way God reveals Himself. I have no name or explanation for it. We may call it the "still, small voice" or the impress of His spirit on us. But I can testify that there are times, perhaps rare times, when you feel you have received a direct word from Him. Samuel heard God directly.

The natural sciences seek to know the true world *about* man. Anthropology and sociology seek to know the true world *of* man. Politics and government seek to know the true world *for* man. Psychology seeks to know the true world *in* man. Philosophy summarizes the truth of the *life* of man. Religion is not only concerned with the past and the present of man, but is also concerned with the world yet *before* and *beyond* man.

CAN WE KNOW THE WILL OF GOD?

When I was studying psychology in college I worked out a number of word tests which I would use on my congregations. For example, say to a person the word "Christmas" and ask that person the first word which comes into his mind. I would get such answers as Santa Claus, decorations, gifts, etc. Rarely would Christ be mentioned. So I would conclude we had commercialized and paganized the Lord's birthday. I think the test was valid, with some limitations.

Well, let's try it on ourselves. I will name a phrase and check your first thought. "Will of God." What does that bring to your mind? The death of a loved one, or some great disaster, or severe suffering from some incurable disease, or some hard sacrifice. Most people will think of some dark picture in relation to the will of God.

Perhaps one cause is our Lord's prayer in Gethsemane, "Nevertheless not my will, but thine be done" (LUKE 22:32). And from His surrender to God's will we see Christ walking up Calvary and being nailed to a cross. So God's will and crosses come to be synonymous terms for us.

However, we can go back further. There was Job. He lost his wealth, his children were killed, he suffered in body, and his wife deserted him. Job associated all those disasters with God, so he says, "The Lord gave, and the Lord hath taken away; blessed be the name of the Lord" (JOB 1:21). So, when our hearts are broken we say, "It is the Lord's will." Naturally we shrink from such a will.

It seems to be a general belief that the will of God is to make things distasteful for us, like taking bad tasting medicine when we are sick, or going to the dentist. Yet we think we would be much happier if we disregarded God's will. We never say, "No, I forever turn my back on God's will." But we do say, "For the time being I will back my own judgment and follow my own will."

Somebody needs to tell us that sunrise is also God's will. There is the time of harvest, the harvest which will provide food and clothes for us, without which life could not be sustained on earth. God ordered the seasons; they are His will. In fact, the good things in life far outweigh the bad. There are more sunrises than cyclones.

I live comfortably during the winter in an automatically steam-heated house. Long before I was born God stored up the gas in the ground which is now being piped into my home for my good. I might say that cold winter freezes are God's will, but I must also know that the warmth God has provided is also His will. Whether you shrink from His will or gratefully surrender to it depends on how you look at it.

Jesus said, "Thy will be done in earth, as it is in heaven." "As in heaven," He said. What do you think of when the word "heaven" comes to your mind? You think of peace, plenty, perfect joy, the absence of pain and suffering and tears. John saw it all and recorded his vision in Revelation 21. That is exactly what we want here and now in our own lives.

Jesus says that is God's will for us.

Before you can pray, "Thy will be done," you must believe it is the best and happiest way. However, sometimes we surrender to the immediate, while God considers life as a whole. For example, here are two boys in school. The will of the teacher is that they spend hours in hard studying. One of the boys rebels against the unpleasant work. He wants to be happy, so he goes to a picture show. Maybe he quits school altogether to go his carefree way.

The other boy sticks to his studies, difficult though they may be. Look at those same two boys ten or twenty years later. The carefree boy is now bound and limited by his own ignorance. He endures hardships and embarrassments caused by his lack of training. The other boy is freer, happier, and finds life easier and more rewarding because he was properly prepared.

There was Joseph, the darling of his father Jacob's heart. Home was for him a place of great joy. But jealousy welled up in his brothers, who put Joseph in a dark well, and later sold him into slavery. Later those same brothers stood before him in need. Joseph said to them: "Be not grieved, nor angry with yourselves, that ye sold me hither: for God did send me before you to preserve life" (GENESIS 45:5).

Surely Joseph's way was hard. But he kept his faith, never giving up, and at the end he could look back and see, as we read in *Hamlet*, "There's a divinity that shapes our ends." Out of the surrender of our Lord in Gethesame did come a cross, but beyond the cross lay an empty tomb and a redeemed world.

Sometimes it is not God who leads us through deep valleys and dark waters. It may be man's ignorance and folly. But even then we can feel His presence, for out of our mistakes God can make something beautiful. God did not bring Job's tragedies. But because of Job's faith God could use those tragedies for Job's final good. It is wonderful what God can do with a broken heart when we give Him all the pieces.

Not only is God's way the best and happiest, it is also within our reach. Many shrink from God's will because of a fear that God will ask them to do more than they can do. There was the man of one talent who buried it in the earth. In explaining his failure, his not even trying, he said to his master: "Lord, I knew thee that thou art an hard man . . . and I was afraid, and went and hid thy talent in the earth" (MATTHEW 25:24,25).

He was afraid of unreasonable demands by his master. He felt that even his best could not please his master. There are some things we cannot do. Not many of us can be great artists. Conspicuous leadership is beyond the reach of most. We could list thousands of things we cannot do.

But of one thing we can be sure, we can do the will of God. Moses thought he couldn't. When God told him to lead the children of Israel out of bondage he made excuses. He sincerely felt it was beyond his abilities. But he did it. With complete faith and confidence, you can pray, "Thy will be done," because God is a loving father who knows His children better than they know themselves. He wants our best, but He expects no more.

To pray, "Thy will be done," is really an enlistment for action. In 1792 William Carey preached a sermon on the text: "Enlarge the place of thy tent, and let them stretch forth the curtains of thine habitations: spare not, lengthen thy cords, and strengthen thy stakes" (ISAIAH 54:2).

It was one of the most influential sermons ever preached on this earth, because the result was the birth of the Baptist Missionary Society, the story of which a hundred books could not begin to tell. In that sermon Carey made his famous statement: "Expect great things from God, attempt great things for God."

But here is the important point. He not only preached about missions, but he also gave up all he had and went himself to India as a missionary. He prayed literally, "in earth as it is in heaven." He meant the whole earth, and he dedicated his life in answer to his own prayer.

The assurance that you are within the will of God does more to eliminate the fears and worries of life than any other one thing. I quote Dante, "In His will is our peace." Surrender to His will takes the dread out of tomorrow. We know, absolutely we know, that if we do His will today, tomorrow will be according to His will. I am not a fatalist. Instead I can say with the Psalmist, "I have not seen the righteous forsaken" (37:25). Obedience to His will today means that God assumes the responsibility for our tomorrow.

Actually, God's will is on earth. It is operating in your very life. For example, you did not decide in what century you would be born. You were not free to choose who your parents would be. The color of your skin, your sex, your physical appearance, all were decided by a higher will, God's will.

And God's will is in operation in our lives. There is a purpose for your life. I believe no person is an accident. Before you were born on the earth you existed in the mind of God. You can rebel against God, but ultimately you will be totally defeated. You can endure life as it comes and find no joy and peace in it. Or you can choose the will of God and make His will your will.

As Tennyson put it: "Our wills are ours, we know not how; our wills are ours, to make them thine."

How can I know the will of God for my life? Many will never know, because God does not reveal Himself to triflers. No one can walk into His holy presence on hurrying feet. If you merely pray, "Lord, this is my will, I hope you will approve," you are wasting your breath. Only those who sincerely want God's will, and have faith enough in Him to dedicate themselves to His will, can ever know it. To pray, "Lord, show me Thy will, and if I like it I will accept it," is a futile prayer. You must accept it before you know it. Whether or not you can do that depends on what opinion you have of God.

What is it we want of God—a house, an automobile, some money in the bank, food to eat and clothes to wear, physical health? Surely we want that, and God wants us to have it. He grows trees to make lumber; He put metals in the earth to make automobiles; He put fertility in the soil grow our food. Within the world He created there are cures for every disease, and one by one men are finding them. When we get these things, are we satisfied and have we no further need for God?

A coin represents service. But unless it is spent it accomplishes nothing. Now there are a lot of fine and good people who are not doing anything as far as service to God is concerned. They are like the man who buried his talents in the ground or the fig tree that produced no fruit. The highest purpose of man is to serve God. If one is not using his talents for God, then he is lost. As far as the work of God is concerned, many people are out of circulation.

GOD'S GUIDANCE

When we decide as Christ did, "... nevertheless not my will, but thine, be done" (LUKE 22:42), it brings happy peace into our lives. That is true, for one reason, because it takes away from us the fear of getting lost in life. Some time ago I was in another city and a friend offered to bring me home in his little two-seater airplane. On the way we suddenly realized we were off course and were lost. We could see no landmarks to guide us, the ground below was rough, and there was no place to land. There was the fear of running out of gas. There was no radio in the plane to check our course. For a time, life for us was a very uncomfortable experience.

On the other hand, not long ago I was flying in one of our big commercial airliners. We were in weather so cloudy that even the wing tips were invisible. I was up front talking with one of the pilots. I asked, "How do you know you are on the right track?" He told me to listen in over his earphones. I could distinctly hear the radio beam. Even though the pilot could not see thirty feet ahead, that invisible beam guided him straight to his field. He had no fear of getting lost.

It is fascinating to study the migration of birds. Take, for example, the Pacific Golden Plover. Those birds are hatched in the northlands of Alaska and Siberia. Before the young ones are old enough to fly great distances, the old birds desert them and fly far away to the Hawaiian Islands. The young birds are left behind to grow strong enough to follow their parents.

One day these birds rise into the sky and set their course out over the Pacific. They have never made that journey before and they must cross two thousand miles of ocean, with no marks to guide them. During this trip they have not even one opportunity to stop for rest or food and frequently they encounter high winds and storms. Yet unerringly they fly straight to those tiny specks in the Pacific, the Hawaiian Islands.

How do you explain the flight of these birds? Surely God has provided them something akin to our radio beams, something they can follow without getting lost. And I firmly believe God has made the same provisions for mankind. When our lives are in harmony with His will, even though we cannot see the way ahead, we have an instinctive sense of the right direction and, with courage and confidence, we move steadily ahead through life, without any fear of getting lost, knowing that through the storms and uncertainties, we shall come to the right place at last. That is a wonderful assurance to possess. "In all thy ways acknowledge him, and he shall direct thy paths" (PROVERBS 3:6).

NEW LIFE

As I write this I can see a man out in the yard raking up the leaves. It makes me sad. I think I have never enjoyed the leaves more than this fall.

My study has large windows on three sides, and through those windows I can see up and down lovely Fairview Road in Atlanta. Surely the trees are no more colorful anywhere and their beautiful profusion of fall color has been food for my soul. It was Charles Kingsley who called beauty "God's handwriting"; and seeing the beauty of the trees, I do not see how any person in his right mind can fail to believe in God.

But now the leaves have lost their beauty and it seems the trees are saying, "There is no use for me to hold on to you any longer." One by one the leaves fall to the ground to become nothing but trash. So the man comes to rake them up to be burned or carried away by the garbage collector to some dumping place. The trees are left bare and ugly, like skeletons.

Thinking of this has brought to mind a shocking statement I read about God. This writer said, "There is a sense in which we ought to think of God as a Celestial Garbage Collector." That seems a terrible thing to say. However, the writer went on to explain that life could not be kept pure and clean without God. Things in our lives that were beautiful were somehow allowed to die, and one by one we dropped them. But to get rid of our broken dreams, our soiled ideals, our stained consciences, is not so easy. They become garbage in our lives with a stench in our nostrils.

As I look at the trees, my mind runs months ahead. Now they are bare, but after winter comes the spring. On the limbs of the tree will burst forth new life, bringing buds and blossoms and fruit and more leaves. The tree will become beautiful and appealing again. It will feel no shame as men gaze upon it; proudly it will stretch itself toward the heavens and stand straight and tall.

He is more, much more than a "Celestial Garbage Collector"—He is the one who said, ". . . I am come that they might have life, and that they might have it more abundantly" (JOHN 10:10). Under His power, we receive a new chance at life. Surely we can believe that God, who does that for the trees, would do no less for His own children.

PROFANING GOD'S NAME

There are at least three ways we profane God's name. First, by our language. We have all kinds of maniacs, but one of the most common types we have in America is "swearomaniacs." It is alarming how our language is being filled with profanity. Many of our modern novels I would enjoy reading, but they contain such vile language that I will not read them because I do not want those words in my mind. The word "hell" has become one of our most common words. We say, "It is cold as hell," "It is hot as hell," "It is raining like hell," etc., etc.

One man came in to see me recently who I thought used the word correctly. He said, "Preacher, I am in a helluva shape," and he was. Hell is down, not up, and to fill my mind with hell and the language of hell degrades my very soul.

The word "profane" comes from two Latin words—"pro" meaning in front of and "fane" meaning temple. A profane word is one you would not use in church, and that is a mighty good way to judge the language we use.

Second, we take God's name in vain by not taking Him seriously. We admit there is a God, but our belief is merely lip service. Jesus said, "Whosoever heareth these sayings of mine, *and doeth them* . . ." (MAT-THEW 7:24). To talk about God and not to live like God is profanity worse than vile language. Belief that does not make a radical difference in life is mere sham and hypocrisy. As Elton Trueblood put it, "An empty, meaningless faith may be worse than none."

A third way we take God's name in vain is by refusing His fellowship and His help. If I say a man is my friend, yet never want to be with him and do not call on him when I need his help, then I am lying when I use the word "friend." If I believe in a mechanic, then I will go to him when my car needs attention. If I believe in a physician I will call him when I become sick. Yet, when Adam and Eve sinned, they ran and hid from God. Their descendants have been doing likewise ever since.

Instead of sleeping pills, a lot of people need an old-fashioned period of repentance. Instead of a new drug, a lot of us need an experience of forgiveness. We need to get right with God and with our own conscience.

PICTURES FOR THE MIND

I wish I were an artist. I would like to paint four pictures and hang them where I would see them every day. Not being able to paint those pictures on canvas, I have made an effort to put them clearly on the screen of my mind.

The first picture shows five thousand hungry people. Standing in their midst is He who always is concerned about human need. In His hands is the little boy's lunch. He might have complained about having so little when He needed so much. Instead of complaining, He lifts up His eyes to God and gives thanks.

The next picture shows this same Christ at a table with twelve men. It seemed that everything was lost and nothing had been gained. In His hand is a piece of bread which He will use as an example of His body and how it will be broken. He might have become panicky or bitter. Instead, the Bible tells us, "He took bread, and gave thanks" (LUKE 22:19).

The third picture shows a ship in the midst of a raging storm at sea. On board were two hundred and seventy-six people. For fourteeen days they had been blown by the storm and now it seemed they might be dashed on the rocks. They were terrified. Then Paul stood up and before the people "took bread, and gave thanks to God" (ACTS 27:35).

The fourth picture shows a little band of people who had just the year before come to America, a new and a strange land. During that year half of their families had died. They were facing a hard winter in New England. Savages were all about them. They had produced a very meager harvest. But in spite of their hard experiences, they knelt to thank God for their blessings.

I wish every person who complains could see those pictures. I wish they could be seen by those who have given up and quit, feeling their resources to be insufficient for their needs, and also by those who are in trouble, or those who have suffered and lost. There is marvelous power in the experience of genuine thanksgiving.

4

Your Life Should Be Full

We must remember who we are. The Bible tells us how God made man out of the dust of the earth. We are also told that our bodies will go back to dust. The Bible also tells us that God breathed into man "the breath of life; and man became a living soul." Don't let your dust make you forget your soul. Remember who you are.

A LIFETIME TO GROW

Whenever I see a baby, I think: "Here is a perfect human being. This little one has never said or thought or done anything that is wrong. It is absolutely perfect." But suppose that baby remained as it is? As time went on, that would be a great tragedy. The glory of a little baby is that it has a lifetime before it in which to grow and develop. There is almost no greater tragedy on this earth than a retarded child, one who never attains true growth and maturity. So, in the Christian life, we are never concerned altogether with what we are; our greater concern is what we may become, and that is what our dreams are all about.

GOD'S PLAN FOR YOUR LIFE

No person is born by accident. God has a plan and a purpose for every life. We have the freedom to rebel against God's plan, or to accept it and live according to His will. The choice is ours but the plan is God's. And blessed is the person who knows God's will for his life and accepts it. But how can we know His will for our lives? That is a question we want answered. Let me briefly give some helpful suggestions.

1. Consider the character of God. God is righteous and holy and He never wills anything that is contrary to His nature. God would never compromise His character to gain an end, no matter how good the end might be. If there is the slightest wrong in the action, it is not God's will.

2. Consider the circumstances of your life. We do not believe God wills tragedy, loss and disappointment, but we do believe that God uses circumstances to the furthering of His purpose. Let us capture the truth that Whittier expressed

> I know not what the future hath
> Of marvel or surprise,
> Assured alone that life and death
> His mercy underlies.

No matter what happens, God can use it to further His plan and purposes for our lives. Instead of giving up in despair, seek the answer to how your life experiences and circumstances can be used in the will of God.

3. Consider three definite ways in which you can receive God's message directly to you. (a) Through prayer. Every decision should be prayed about, remembering that prayer means talking to God and also listening to God. Take time for both. (b) Through the reading of His Word, the Bible. There is revealed the fundamental truths for living. (c) Through your conscience. If you will listen, you will hear the "still small voice" inside you.

4. Consider your consecration to God. The Bible tells us, "In all thy ways acknowledge him." That must come first. Then follows, "and he shall direct thy paths" (PROVERBS 3:6). That means that we must have faith enough in God to accept Him and His direction, then He will give us that direction. But we cannot fool God. He knows whether or not we have surrendered our wills to His will.

Life is so constituted that no person can stand still. Either we are progressing or we are dying. Either we are getting better or we are getting worse. Either we are helping ourselves or we are hurting ourselves.

DEVELOPING A CHRISTIAN LIFE

How can I develop my Christian life? In answer, I suggest seven definite practices which, if performed regularly and sincerely, will cause one to grow as Jesus grew: "In wisdom and stature, and in favour with God and man" (LUKE 2:52).

1. Remember that Christianity is a religion of fellowship. As John Wesley put it, "The Bible knows nothing of a solitary religion." This means

that one must make friends with other Christians, for from each other we catch faith and inspiration. The most adequate Christian fellowship is the church. It is not perfect but is the best to be found. So you will want to belong to some church, attend the worship services regularly, contribute a fair share of your income to its support, find a place of service in the church, and pray for it daily. The church was established by Christ and if you love Him, you will love His church.

2. Read your Bible regularly. The Bible is different from any book on earth. As Moody said, "I know the Bible is inspired because it inspires me." It is well to begin with Matthew and go on through the four Gospels. And the important thing is not how many chapters we read, but how well we digest the part we do read. I suggest reading only a few verses at a time and thinking meditatively upon them. Memorize some of the verses—hide the Word in your heart. Never let a day pass without reading the Bible.

3. Learn how to pray. The best way to learn is by doing. Prayer is an art and the more we pray the more powerful prayer becomes in our lives. Of course, one can pray any time, anywhere, but to pray most effectively, have definite times of prayer. Pray before each meal. Pray before you go to bed. Pray when you first awaken in the morning. God answers every prayer. Sometimes His answer is "Yes," sometimes it is "No," sometimes it is "Wait." But His answer always comes and it is always the best answer for you.

4. Be a tither. That means, give 10 percent of your income to the Lord's work. We should tithe for two reasons: first, it is God's command; second, tithing brings greater blessings. I have never know a tither who was not helped by it. I have never known a tither who was not happy. Read MALACHI 3:10.

5. Rely on the help of God in your daily life. St. Paul said, "I can do all things through Christ which strengtheneth me" (PHILIPPIANS 4:13). The Christian life is a partnership with Christ and when we realize that, all thoughts of despair, hopelessness and defeat are driven out of our minds. We learn to think in terms of victory and we do not worry about what might happen to us. When we take hold of the power of Christ, we can let go of those inner tensions and fears and develop confidence and courage. This partnership lifts us above the circumstances of life and causes us to be our best where we are.

6. Remember always the emblem of the Christian. Jesus said, "By this shall all men know that ye are my disciples, if ye have love one to another" (JOHN 13:35). A Christian does not carry a grudge, neither can

a Christian hold in his heart any wrong spirit toward any other person. 7. Always be a witness for Christ. We witness by our lives, our deeds and our words. And a Christian is ever seeking in every way possible to win others to Christ and His way.

Follow these seven steps. Your own faith will steadily grow and your life will also be a blessing to others.

THE HIGHEST ROOM

Think of your mind as being a house with several rooms. One room of your house is your office, which represents your daily work. One may spend all of his time in that room, and never get away from the worries and problems of making a living. Another room in the house is the kitchen, in which your meals are prepared. One may live his life on the animal level, thinking only of the satisfaction of his physical desires. Underneath the house is the cellar, which might indicate the dingy, dark areas, the secret desires for wrong, lust, and all of the other destructive emotions of men. One can live on that level. Above is the attic, which stores an accumulation of your past. One can live with old griefs and fears, old worries and regrets. In some houses, however, above the attic there is a room to which one can climb, high above the ground, which looks out toward the heavens. No matter where one's body may happen to be—walking along the street, working at the job, standing in the midst of a crowd—one can climb into this mental room high above and there commune with Him who is the Highest.

You never live until you begin to live for something.

DIALOGUE

Jesus said, "Consider the lilies of the field, how they grow; . . . even Solomon in all his glory was not arrayed like one of these" (MATTHEW

6:28,29). Jesus was pointing out one of the humblest of God's creatures. He did not refer to some beautiful flower growing in a magnificent palace; instead it was a common little wildflower of the field. Supppose we talk to the little lily and seek to find out its secret: "Lily, Jesus said you are more glorious than Solomon. How did you attain your glory? Do you have a magic formula?"

"No," says the lily, "I simply grew."

"Then you were not always the glorious creature that you are now?"

The lily replies, "No, I once was a bulb. Then I was planted in the ground. Out of me a little green shoot came, and little by little I just grew. But I want you to know that I did not grow all by myself. I was planted in the soil that God provided. His sun warmed and lighted my way. He sent the gentle showers to give me moisture. And I breathed the air that He created. God took care of my every need."

If one listens to the lily, he may hear the lily saying, "There was a time when I resented the fact that I was nothing but a little lily. I looked at the sunflower, so tall and straight, and I wanted to be like that. Or I could see the great oak tree over yonder, and I thought about how long the tree would live, and I wanted to be a tree. But then I realized that God made me a lily, and that was all that I could be. So I set out to be the finest lily that I could be."

As we keep listening, we may hear the lily saying, "There is something else God taught me. When I first began to grow into a lily, I was very happy. Then the bees and the birds would come along and take some of my sweetness. The workers in the field would walk by and look upon me. The wind would steal some of my perfume. I began to be afraid that all I had would be gone. I felt as if I should veil my face and keep all I had, but when I did that, I began to wither and die. And then it was I learned that the fine art of living is the fine art of giving."

Then the lily might look at one of us and speak very seriously: "God has done all of this for me, and yet I am going to live for such a short time. You heard for yourself Jesus' words: 'Wherefore, if God so clothe the grass of the field, which to day is, and to morrow is cast into the oven, shall he not much more clothe you . . . ?' You are made in the likeness of God. You are His child. You can think God's thoughts after Him. You can render God's services. You are made with a soul that will live eternally; when your life is over, you will be with God in His house. When you look at me and realize how much God has done for me, just think about how much more He will do for you."

Jesus is saying to each one of us: "When you look about you in God's creation, and see what God has done for all of His creatures, and then consider how much more important a human being is, is it not reasonable to have faith and confidence in Him?"

We sometimes think that our lives are determined by the circumstances that surround us. Actually, the opposite is true. The kind of person you are determines the circumstances about you. If you want a better life, the place to change is inside yourself.

When life is not all we want, some choose the color of blue which stands for a depressed, despondent spirit. Some choose the color of yellow. They run away from life in a cowardly fashion. But others choose red, which stands for courage. "Yes, thank God, I can choose the color."

EQUIPPED FOR LIFE

Concentrate on your powers instead of your problems. I read the other day about a group of scientists who met to discuss the possibility of building a machine with the powers of a human brain. But they gave up the idea because it would be too great a task.

They said that the human brain has ten million nerve centers and for every one of those ten million centers there would have to be an electronic tube. You have a radio with five or ten tubes; think about one with ten million tubes.

It would take a building equal to a fifteen-hundred room hotel to house it. They said that a machine with the intelligence of an ordinary earthworm would require ten thousand tubes. Even if a brain could be built, it would cost millions and millions of dollars; but God made one and put it in your head. Yet we only use 10 percent of our brain power.

Then look at your hands. We possess many wonderful tools but nothing has ever been equal to the powers of a human hand. It is wonderful to think about what a hand can do. So, with a brain and two hands, all of us are pretty well equipped to meet whatever may come along. Instead of wishing for a buried treasure in some form, we would do a lot better to start thinking how we can better use what we already have.

But, as powerful as a person is, there is a still greater power that we can also use. Whenever he became a little shaky, Martin Luther used to go out into his garden and sing: "A mighty fortress is our God, a bulwark never failing; Our helper He, amid the flood of mortal ills prevailing." That always prepared him to face with confidence whatever might come. He knew that so long as there is a God, he could feel secure.

THE TUGBOAT AND THE DAM

Just outside of Florence, Alabama, is a high bluff overlooking the Tennessee River. On top of the bluff is a lovely little park. I was in Florence for a revival, and one afternoon a friend took me out to that little park. It was wonderful to sit there watching that beautiful river. Just above us we could see one of those great hydro-electric dams built by TVA.

Presently I saw a tugboat coming up stream towing a barge. It seemed to be huffing and puffing with all its might against the current. I asked my friend where the tug would stop. He told me it wouldn't stop. Instead, it would go up into the lake above. I wanted to see that, because I had never known of a tugboat that could fly and I did not know how else it could get over that big dam.

My friend explained that they had built a series of locks around the dam. I watched the tug tow the barge into the first lock, when its puffing ceased. The gates were closed below and opened above, and as the water came in gradually the boat began to rise. Then it moved into the second lock and was lifted to a higher level. Finally, it had been lifted to the level of the lake and then, under its own power again, it could move on.

As I saw that, I, too, was lifted. I thought about how we huff and puff upstream against the swift currents of life. Sometimes we come to places where we cannot go on under our own power. Then I thought of a verse in Deuteronomy, "The eternal God is thy refuge, and underneath are the everlasting arms" (33:27). There is such a thing as resting back on the lifting power of God.

JESUS' FORMULA FOR LIVING

Jesus gave us a formula for power in living. He said, "Have faith in God. For verily I say unto you, That whosoever shall say unto this mountain, Be thou removed, and be thou cast into the sea; and shall not doubt in his heart, but shall believe that those things which he saith shall come to pass; he shall have whatsoever he saith" (MARK 11:12,23).

Look at that formula: "Faith in God"—not in ourselves, but in God. "For verily"—He emphasizes the fact that what He is about to say will be hard to believe but it is the truth. "Whosoever"—that means any person; it means me, it means you. "Say unto this mountain"—that is specific and definite. Select any circumstance of your own life that is standing in your way and this formula will apply. "Be thou removed"— taken out of my way. No longer can it hurt me. "Cast into the sea"— gone forever, complete victory. "Shall not doubt . . . but shall believe" —it is through my own faith that the victory is accomplished. "Shall come to pass"—it really will happen.

MESSAGE FROM THE OCEAN

Recently I spent some weeks at Sea Island, Georgia, the most beautiful and inspiring place I know of anywhere. The homes, trees and flowers there are as lovely as man working with God can make them.

But especially was I fascinated by the sea. I would go to sleep at night to the melody of the breakers coming in upon the shore. I would eat breakfast each morning on the porch looking out across the vastness of the water. Each day I would walk several miles down the beach. I would swim out into the deep and then ride the waves back in.

Sometimes I would become almost overwhelmed with how big the ocean is and how little I am. Looking at the ocean, one almost feels a sense of helplessness. We recall that Lord Byron once wrote

> Roll on, thou deep and dark blue ocean, roll!
> Ten thousand fleets sweep over thee in vain;
> Man marks the earth with ruin,—his control
> Stops with the shore.

As you look at the ocean you realize: here is something bigger than any man, even bigger than all men.

Then you remember that the Bible says, "In his hand are the deep places of the earth . . . The sea is his and he made it" (PSALM 95:4,5). There is One who is bigger than even the ocean. There is a God who is not helpless before it. There is a God who can and does control the sea. Realizing that, your faith is strengthened and you feel serene and unafraid.

As you live by the ocean for a time, there comes a better understanding of life because the two are so much alike. Life itself has a vastness that is beyond the reach of our sight. Just as we are told, "In his hand are the deep places of the earth . . ." also we can say with the psalmist, "I trusted in thee, O Lord . . . My times are in thy hand . . ." (PSALM 31:14,15). We believe nothing can happen in our lives that God cannot handle. That gives us confidence and faith as we think of tomorrow.

There are many parallels between life and the ocean, but one especially impresses me—the coming and going of the tides. The tides go out and are low, the tides come in and are high. There is no power of earth that can prevent the low and high tides. So it is with an individual life—we experience times of low tide and of high tide and there is no way to stop those tides.

If we realize that we will experience low tides of our spirit, then our moments of depression and discouragement lose much of their terror. Even the true saints, those whose lives have been most completely in the hands of God, knew times when things seemed dark and when the shining of God's eternal light was very dim. There are times when we do not have a sense of the fullness of God's power, or the realization of His presence. Then we say even as Christ said, "My God, my God, why hast thou forsaken me" (MATTHEW 27:46).

WHAT THE CREEK SAID

The other day, I flew over a swamp. The plane was low enough so that one could see clearly the water below; it was covered with an ugly green film. That swamp is a breeding place for mosquitoes and vermin of many kinds. There was nothing attractive about it, and it certainly was not an area where one would want to spend much time. That swamp is fed by a creek that runs up into the mountains. I am quite familiar with that creek because a number of times I have been up it fishing for rainbow trout. It is a beautiful creek, clear and sparking and pure. Up in the mountains it runs in a rather narrow bed, and many times it is compelled to flow over rocks and rough places. As it flows on down out of hills into the lowlands, the creek says to itself, "I am tired of this restricted narrow life I have been forced to live. I want to spread out and take in more territory." But, in spreading out, it ceases to be the clear, pure creek and becomes a contaminated swamp.

The Christian faith leads one into life rather than away from life.

KEY RING OF PRAYER

I know a man who puts his keys into one of his shoes each night when he goes to bed. The next morning when he dresses to begin a new day, that shoe is the last thing he puts on. He takes out those keys, holds them in his hand and says something like this:

"Lord, this day I will come to certain doors that are locked but I shall use these keys to open those doors. And may I remember this day that there is a key to every situation, a solution to every problem. May I never surrender to one of life's locked doors. Instead, may I use the keys on the key ring of prayer until I find the right key and the door be opened."

THREE PRAYER WORDS

So many people get nothing because they want nothing. Jesus said, "Ask . . . seek . . . knock" (MATTHEW 7:7).

These three "prayer words" in the original Greek are in the present tense, and they call for continuing action. The better translation is "Keep on asking, keep on seeking, keep on knocking." Life is both alike and different from mountain climbing. Alike in that the climber is constantly struggling higher; different in that in life we never reach the top. In life we never arrive because we never run out of heights to climb. The moment we give up the struggle of the climb, we begin to fall back and die.

Someone asked Raphael, "Which is your greatest painting?" He said. "My next one." That is the spirit that made him great.

Notice the order and meaning of these words: "Ask" is first. A child asks its father for something. It is really an admission of helplessness. The child cannot earn it or provide it for himself. The man on the corner who is blind asks for help. He is merely begging, he offers nothing in return. And before God there are many times we can only come asking. However, we are His children and that gives us the right to ask without shame.

"Seek" is the next word. That means asking plus effort. The boy who goes asking for a job is at the same time offering his service. Many of God's gifts come not in the form of pure gold, but in ore to be dug out of the earth. The gold is there, only awaiting our effort. That is as it should be. We don't want to go through life as mere beggars.

"Knock." Jesus told a story of a man who continued to knock on his neighbor's door at midnight until the man inside got up and answered his request (LUKE 11:5-8). Knocking means asking plus effort plus persistence.

No one of us is a single self. Life would be so much simpler if we were. There is our careless self, which drifts along without thinking or trying. There is our passionate self. We do many things as a result of fear, anger, lust or some other passion. There is our greedy self. We forget our obligations, we kill all the love in our hearts, if we let greed have its way. But, thank God, there is also our best self. "To thine own self be true."

THE GOOD SUBSTITUTE

We like football. It is a rough game in which the player takes some hard knocks, but there is a thrill about it. There is the cheering of the crowd, the write-ups in the paper, the satisfaction of playing the game. The hardest position to play on the football team is sitting on the bench. Nobody applauds the bench sitter. All he can do is wait, hoping for a chance to play.

The good substitute remains ready whenever the coach calls. And in the great game of life, it seems that God keeps a lot of people waiting. But be assured He doesn't forget us, and He would have us remain free of bitterness. It is ours to do our best under the circumstances and leave the rewards to Him.

ACCEPTING OURSELVES

One of the secrets of success and happiness in life is being willing to accept ourselves as we are. You could not choose who your parents would be. You had nothing to say about the color of your skin, whether you would be a man or woman, whether you would be short or tall. A pine tree will be a pine tree until it dies and goes back to dust. It can never be anything else.

So it is with each of us. We are not responsible for being the persons we are. God made us who we are and that is fixed forever. We might wish God had made us differently, but no amount of wishing can make much change. Thus, our business in life is to take ourselves in hand and see what we can make out of the selves we are. And in spite of our limited and handicapped selves, we can make a contribution to the world.

POSSIBILITIES COME IN PAIRS

Every possible blessing is also a possible pain. Here is an illustration. I bought roller skates for my children. I remember that I found great joy in skating and I wanted my children to enjoy it too. However, when one puts on skates, he also greatly increases the possibility of falling and getting hurt.

I watched my children when they first tried to skate. They would fall on the hard concrete and it would hurt and sometimes they would cry. In that instance, would you say that I caused their pain? In a sense I did; but by giving them skates I also increased the possibility of joy and pleasure in their lives. By giving them skates I was allowing them to get hurt, but it certainly was not my will. It would have been very different if I had gone out and banged their heads against the concrete.

A boy is killed in an automobile wreck. When his father allowed him to drive the car he certainly did not intend that the boy be killed. The father might have said, "It is possible for one to be killed in an automobile wreck. Therefore, because I love you I will not let you drive or even ride in a car." On the other hand, the father wanted the boy to have the advantage and pleasure of the car, and thus he permitted him to drive.

God has provided for us wonderful things for our joy. Take love, for example. Love brings life's greatest blessings but it also brings life's greatest pains. God gave men and women the capacity to love each other. We marry and build our homes. Into our homes come children and then a new love is born into our hearts. Then something happens to one we love and our hearts are broken. But that is just one of the prices we must pay for love.

God gave us the capacity to dream, to hope and to aspire. But sometimes we do not realize our dreams; our hopes are dashed to the ground; our fondest ambitions are thwarted. Then we know the pain of disappointment and frustration. On the other hand, we also have the possibility of knowing the thrill of achievement. In order to have the possibility of one we must be willing to accept the possibility of the other.

A team goes out on the baseball field to play a game. They give their best but they are beaten, and defeat is hard to bear. They could have avoided their defeat by not playing the game. But also they would have denied themselves the chance to win. If one plays the game, then he must accept both the possibilities of winning and of losing.

Study life and you will see that life's possibilities come in pairs:

goodness and evil, short and tall, strong and weak, hot and cold, black and white—and also, pain and pleasure. The existence of one carries with it the possibility of the other. If there were no pain, then there would be no pleasure in life either.

Sooner or later, all of us become the person we see ourselves to be. If you develop creative faith in yourself, eventually your faith will recreate you. If your mind is obsessed by thoughts of insecurity and inadequacy, it is because you have allowed such thoughts to dominate your thinking over a period of time. The only way to overcome those thoughts is by putting into your mind a positive pattern of ideas.

Let the physical body be wounded and immediately the healing forces of nature go to work. A city is bombed and destroyed, but out of the wreckage a new city is built. The will to live is deeply planted within all life, both natural and human.

YOUR OWN IDENTITY

Before you were born, you existed in the mind of God. He decided that the world needed you at a certain time—that there is something for you to do that is different from what any other person will do. Everything God made has its own peculiar identity. There are billions of blades of grass, but no two alike. No two snowflakes have ever been identical.

No person who ever existed is exactly like you. Even the print of your little finger is separate and distinct. It should lift you to a new realization of importance to know that of all the billions of people the earth has known, there is only one of you.

DRESS UP A LIFE

Dressing up the Christmas tree every year is a great experience. When I was a boy we used long popcorn strings. That was not so fancy, but I thought at the time it made a mighty pretty tree.

To decorate our trees today we use all kinds of gay lights, tinsel, artificial snow and icicles, colored bulbs and an electric star in the top. It is a glowing thing.

But when God decorates a tree He does it differently. Take an apple tree, for example. He doesn't come down some night and tie a lot of leaves and blossoms on His tree. Instead, He sends the sunshine and rain and puts food in the good earth, and the tree develops a healthy and vigorous life *inside*. Then the leaves, blossoms, and apples just come naturally.

And it is a good time to think about the best way to dress up a life. You might call it the development of your personality.

The old Pharisees insisted on the Christmas tree method—a tacking on from the outside process. They keep adding all kinds of laws and regulations of things one must and must not do.

Today we have personality experts, charm schools, and "self-help" books. But they are neither new nor modern. They are simply a carry-over of that old Pharisaism.

The greatest Student of human nature who ever lived told these Pharisees they were going about it in the wrong way. He wanted people to live the good life, too. In fact, He came to fulfil the law. But you can't develop this good life by just adding more things to do and not to do.

"Whatsovever things are true . . . honest . . . just . . . pure . . . lovely . . . of good report . . . think on these things" (PHILIPPIANS 4:8). Plant such things firmly and deep in your thinking. Let them drive the unlovely things out of your mind and you need not be concerned about developing a lovable and winsome personality. It will come naturally, the apple tree method.

5

Hallmarks of Christian Living

Stand at the seashore, and watch the tide go out and the tide come in. There is no power on earth great enough to stop the tide, and that principle operates all through life: what goes out, comes in. Send out love, and love comes back. Send out hate, and hate comes back. Send out mercy, mercy comes back. What we give, we get.

LIFE IS FOR SHARING

Recently I spent nearly a week in a little cottage far back in the mountains. I never enjoyed anything in my life as much as I enjoyed the first two days there. I went to bed at dark and slept for ten hours. I sat on the porch and looked at the beautiful mountains. I was several miles away from a telephone. No newspaper was delivered to my door. Nobody came around to see me. There was no mail to answer.

But after a couple of days I caught up on my sleep and I got restless. I walked around through the woods, but just walking without going anywhere didn't appeal to me very long. I wanted something to do. I wanted to be with other people. God did not make us just to enjoy His world. He made us to work in His world. And in the sharing with Him of the continual creation we find our life. When we cease to be a part of the creative work of God we soon die.

One day Jesus condemned a fig tree to death because it produced no fruit. Some people seemed shocked that Christ would use His power for destructive purposes. But such is the very basic law of life. When we cease to bear fruit we die.

TAKE A LITTLE HONEY

"Take a little honey." Those were the words of Jacob to his sons when they were going down into Egypt to buy food. They took many gifts—balm, spices, myrrh, nuts and money. But wise old Jacob added, "Take a little honey" (GENESIS 43:11).

Honey is sweet, gentle and kind, and without those qualities no person can really succeed in the business of living.

I know people who have taken with them on the journey of their lives ability, training, initiative, ambition, faith, and so many good things. Yet they failed because they forgot kindness. If they had just been a little sweeter in spirit what a difference it would have made.

A hog will eat acorns under a tree day after day, never looking up to see where they came from. Some people are like that—but others are led through their blessings to realize the love of their heavenly Father.

PRINCIPLES OF HAPPINESS

We would do well to begin living by the eight principles Christ said would make us happy.

Poor in spirit—not satisfied with ourselves, but ever looking upward.

Mourn—a heart that never feels sorrow will never feel joy. Through grief we grow strong as we let God into our hearts through the broken places.

Meek—we neither rebel against life nor submit to our misfortunes. Rather, we accept life as it is, and we cooperate with the will and plan of God.

Hunger and thirst after righteousness—our greatest ambition is not how much we can possess, but how right our lives can become.

Merciful—we keep clean of grudges and the poisons of hate, anger, jealousy, and bitterness. Mercy overlooks the little things and forgives the large things.

Pure in heart—we set a worthy goal for our lives. As we become attached to some high purpose, and give ourselves to it, we do find God.

Peacemakers—there are so many occasions to give ourselves to the ministry of God's peace.

Persecuted for righteousness' sake—the high purpose of our lives lifts us above pain and those who would hurt and harm us.

These, said Jesus, are the steps to happiness—to more than mere happiness: to blessedness!

One can steal money and be sent to prison. But it is far worse for a bad temper to steal the peace and happiness of a home. One might set off a stick of dynamite under a church, and he would be prosecuted for it. But it is a greater crime for an unbridled tongue or a sulky spirit to blast the brotherhood and fellowship of the church.

One of the finest lessons people can learn in life is to be able to disagree without being disagreeable.

WHAT-ARE-YOU-GOING-TO-DO QUESTIONS

I have a close friend who became the pastor of some little country churches. The preacher before him had told the people of their sins in emphatic language. He was one of those "fearless" preachers, but the little churches had about died under his ministry.

My friend took a different approach. His very first sermon was on the text, "Whosoever heareth these sayings of mine, and doeth them" (MATTHEW 7:24). He "accentuated the positive." At the close of his sermon he passed out sheets of paper on which were written four questions:

1. What are you going to do this month to make you a better Christian? He got such answers as, "I am going to read the Gospel of Matthew," "I am going to speak kindly to every person I meet," etc.

2. "What are you going to do this month to make your home happier?" One listed daily family prayers, another said he would clean up his yards and make them look better. One man would not say, but at the end of the month he told the minister to come around and see. It was a kitchen sink. He explained that his wife had always "toted" water from the spring on the hill. During the month he had run a pipe from the spring into the kitchen, and now the wife had all the water she needed. As a result, she could rest more and feel happier.

3. Instead of complaining about their lack of support of the church, the minister asked, "What are you going to do this month to make your church better?" They listed such things as regular attendance, inviting others, contributing more, etc. One man said he would try to sing better.

4. What are you going to do this month to help your community? Some of the answers were: "I am going to work for better recreational facilities for the young people," "I am going to work for community co-operation," etc.

Every month the minister put before the people a series of "What-are-you-going-to-do" questions. He had very little to say about their sins. But at the end of the year the congregations of the little churches had more than doubled and for the first time these people realized something of the joy and thrill of positive Christian living.

POSITIVE PEACE

What is peace? The mere absence of strife is not peace. At the moment Jesus was speaking of peace there was no war on earth, but neither was there peace. The Roman Empire had forced the world to its knees, and the people had lost both the means and the will to fight.

Peace is a positive force. You may clear some plot of land of every noxious weed, but that will not make of it a garden. It will be only a barren field. It becomes a garden when flowers are growing there. The prophet of old reminds us that just to break up our swords and spears is not enough. Those swords must become plowshares and the spears pruning hooks (MICAH 4:3).

To have peace in both the world and our souls, not only must hate, suspicion and fear be rooted out. Also must love, joy, patience and understanding be planted and cultivated. Peace is something to be made; thus we must be peacemakers if we are to enter the Kingdom of God.

God did not put all His stars in any one person's sky or plant all His flowers in any one garden. One may feel that God planted only common daisies in his yard and worry about the lovely roses growing in his neighbor's garden. We will not make the daisies of our own lives any prettier by being jealous of the roses in our neighbors' lives.

FOUR ATTITUDES

As you go along through life, somebody will do you wrong. You can count on that. When someone does you wrong, there are four attitudes you may take. First, "If he hurts me, I will hurt him more"; that is vindictive vengeance. Second, "If he hurts me, I will treat him the same";

that is retribution, the old law of an eye for an eye. Third, "If he hurts me, I will ignore him, and have nothing to do with him"; that is indifference, disdain. Fourth, "If he hurts me, I will love him, and serve him"; that is the Christian way, and that is the way that brings reward.

THE DOCTOR'S PRESCRIPTION

A doctor is prescribing for a group of sick people. After examination, he discovers they are filled with poisons that will not only eventually destroy their bodies, but rob them of all the joy and peace of life and eventually destroy their souls. He discovers they are filled with the poisons of envy, jealousy, selfishness and hate. Each one is thinking of himself as more important than any of his fellows. One says he is the finest public speaker. Another claims to be able to look into the future, while another feels he is better educated. Still another claims to do more for other people.

The wise doctor tells them no matter what abilities they may possess or what services they may render, if their hearts are not filled with love, they do not amount to anything. Then he analyzes his prescription of love. The doctor is St. Paul and you can read all this in I CORINTHIANS 13.

Love is not a single thing, but a composite of many things.

1. Love "suffereth long." This is the attitude of love. To be patient means to possess endurance under stress or annoyance. Love works today while it waits for tomorrow.

On the desk of a very fine businessman I saw the motto, "This, too, shall pass." He told me that that motto had saved him many times. No matter how bad the storm may be, if you are sure that one day it will blow out and the sun will shine again, you will never give up.

2. "And is kind." That is the activity of love. Many years ago I learned a little verse by Ella Wheeler Wilcox that has been a constant inspiration to me.

> So many gods, so many creeds,
>   So many paths that wind and wind,
>   When just the art of being kind
> Is all this sad world needs.

A man once said about his sick wife, "There is nothing I would not do for her." One of the neighbors replied, "That is just the trouble. You have been doing nothing for her for forty years."

3. Love "envieth not." As Henry Drummond, who wrote the greatest sermon in existence on this chapter, said, "This is love in competition with others." Envy leads to hate and hate destroys a soul. Love always congratulates.

4. Love is humble—"vaunteth not itself, is not puffed up." Love and conceit are contradictory terms. What God wants is men great enough to be small enough to be used. Love takes a towel, girds itself, and gets on its knees to do a menial task that lesser men are too big to do.

5. "Doth not behave itself unseemly." Love is courteous. Love possesses tact and good manners. The old, old saying is still true: "Politeness is to do and say, the kindest thing in the kindest way." Love never wants to offend, it never demands its rights, it is respectful and is ever mindful of the desires and comforts of others.

6. "Seeketh not her own." The greatest verse in the Bible tells us: "For God so loved the world that he gave. . ." (JOHN 3:16). Love is always more concerned with what it can give than with what it can get. Love is seeking to minister rather than to be ministered unto. Love understands that it is, "Not what we gain but what we give, that measures the worth of the life we live."

7. "Is not easily provoked." Love is good-tempered. This is a lack that many people brag about. They tell you about their temper as if it were a great asset. But it is no credit to be able to get mad.

There are two types of sins—the sins of the body and the sins of the disposition; both are bad but of the two, I would rather be in the company of some prodigal who went to the far country than some elder brother who stayed at home and lived a moral life yet had a bad disposition. Love knows how to keep certain emotions cool.

8. "Thinketh no evil; rejoiceth not in iniquity." Love is not suspicious and never accuses merely on rumor. Love believes the best of every person until proven wrong. And if some person does go wrong, love is not secretly glad and does not gossip about it.

9. "Beareth all things." Love bears its burdens with dignity, continues to believe, never loses hope and endures to the end.

CIRCLES OF LOVE

The way of the world was an eye for an eye and a tooth for a tooth. Hate always led to hate. Wrong always brought revenge. But one day the vicious circle was broken. One called Jesus came offering men a higher way and a better life, but men stood back to mock and to laugh and to crucify.

About His head was a bright circle, and when He uttered the word, "Forgive," that circle of God's love and approval became large enough to include others. A thief on a cross near by stepped inside that circle with Him and in so doing entered Paradise. The circle reaches to my own feet. To stay outside is to know hate, revenge, and destruction. Inside is to know God's healing love and eternally to possess His Kingdom.

Sometimes I look at certain people and I wonder how even God could love them. Then I think of myself, and with even greater wonder do I realize He loves me. Remembering His love for me helps me to obey His command to love my fellow man, no matter what he may have done.

THE CONTAGION OF CHRIST'S LOVE

I recall an experience of mine that illustrates the fact that when Christ comes into the human heart, we can love. I was preaching in a series of revival services. One morning, a lady phoned, asking to see me. She seemed in distress, but I could not possibly free any time for her until after the service that night. I promised to talk with her then. When I did meet her, she was smiling, and so happy that she seemed to bubble over.

I asked, "Are you sure you're the lady who phoned me this morning?"

She said, "Yes, but I don't need your help now, so I won't keep you."

I said, "Lady, when a person has changed as completely as you have, I want to know what happened." So, we sat down in the front pew of the church, and she told me her story.

Her husband had died suddenly, leaving no money nor insurance for the support of his wife and their four children. He did have, however, a small electrical-supply business. In the business was a man the husband had trained for six years, and the woman felt she should carry on the business with that man's help. She had one competitor in that community, and he tried to buy her out, offering only a fraction of what her business was worth. When she wouldn't sell, he became angry, and told her he would force her out of business. He cut prices, and did everything he could against her, yet she held on. Then, one day, the man her husband had trained told her he was quitting. He was going to work for the competitor, who had offered him more money than the woman could pay.

She carried on by herself as best she could, but it was a struggle. Sometimes her children did not have enough to eat. Worse was the hatred she had in her heart against the man who had hurt her. Hate is poison for both our souls and our bodies, and she knew that; yet she could not seem to do anything about it. It was in that situation she had phoned me that morning. That night she arranged for a neighbor to sit with her children, and she came to church to talk with me about it after the service.

My sermon that night was on the cross. I talked about how, through the power of mental television (imagination and memory), we can actually see back across the years. In detail I described His praying in Gethsemane, the coming of the soldiers, the betraying kiss of one He had trusted, and His trials before Herod and Pilate. I told about His humiliation before that mob as they stripped off His clothes, how they drove in the nails, hung Him up to die, and then spat on Him, mocked and ridiculed Him.

I took about forty-five minutes to describe that picture as vividly as I could. Then I said, "Listen! He is about to speak!" We strained our ears and across the centuries His voice came clear and strong, saying, "Father, forgive them." Then I invited those present to come to the altar and pray.

The woman told me that, as she knelt, the only thing she could think of was the man she hated so. She found herself praying for him. She prayed the prayer the Master prayed, and she felt cleansed and whole again. She told me how she had no fear of the future. When Christ comes into our hearts, we can love even as He loved.

One cannot be right with God until he is right with his fellow man. Therefore, any worship of God is meaningless as long as there is an unrepaired human relationship in our hearts.

In a very real sense, we ourselves are broadcasting stations. Through the process of mental telepathy, our thoughts are received by other people. If I have an unloving spirit, my mind picks up that spirit, expresses it in thoughts and sends it out. As some other person receives my thought, perhaps subconsciously, that person begins to develop an unloving spirit toward me. On the contrary, if I broadcast thoughts of love and good will, the other person begins to feel the same way toward me.

TRUST YOUR HEART

I want to set down one of the supreme principles of faith. It is: Don't be afraid to trust your heart. I got it from a young couple who had come to talk with me about their plans for marriage. It seemed that it would be very difficult for this marriage to succeed and I discussed with them some of the obstacles in their path to happiness together.

There were considerable differences in their backgrounds, both financially and socially. They were of different religious faiths, and I pointed out how each could be hurt in the years to come. There were some other problems. I really hoped they would decide to take more time and possibly reconsider.

Finally the girl spoke up. I had much admiration for her because of the circumstances under which I had come to know her. Once I had been on an airplane which ran into a rather heavy storm. In the turbulent air, the plane was pushed around considerably. Some of the passengers got sick and the rest of us got mighty scared. This girl was the stewardess on that plane, and she moved among the passengers with a calmness and courage that was wonderful to see. Now, feeling the threat of some stormy weather which may lie ahead of her flight into matrimony, she was no less calm and her answer was wonderful. She said, "We love each other and we are not afraid to trust our hearts."

THE CALL OF LOVE

Let us never forget that the love of God has moral depth and it makes great demands. We sing silly little songs with titles such as "Somebody Up There Likes Me," and we talk about "The Man Upstairs," and we think of God's love as something that fits into a juke box. But God's love demands high living. When Jesus saw men of great promise giving themselves to fish nets, He said unto them, "Follow me, and I will make you fishers of men" (MATTHEW 4:19). Love calls to the highest life.

A LESSON IN FORGIVENESS

The visitor was very upset. In fact, she told me she was on the verge of a nervous breakdown. She had to force herself to eat, she had difficulty sleeping, and life for her, she said, was just not worth living.

Her husband had been unfaithful to her, but now he was deeply repentant. She did not want to break up her home, yet neither did she feel she could continue living with him. I told her she would have to forgive him and never mention it again. We talked about it, and finally she agreed to do so. We had a prayer together, in which she told God she had forgiven her husband and asked God to forgive him, also.

Then I said, "You must forgive that other woman." She bristled up and almost shouted, "That I will never do. I cannot, and, even if I could, I would not. She is a low, unmentionable creature, and as long as I live I will hate her. For me to forgive her is unthinkable and impossible."

I asked her if she had a television set. She had. I told her she also had one in her mind which was far more wonderful than one that can be bought. With your mental television you can see things that happened long ago. So I suggested that as I named some scenes of a certain drama she watch the pictures on the television screen of her mind. So I named the scenes as follows:

It is late at night as Jesus and eleven disciples are walking in the Garden of Gethsemane. They pause for a prayer together. Then Jesus and three of the men go on a little farther. He tells them to watch while He goes on a little farther by Himself. He is kneeling now by a large rock. She said she could see those scenes in her mind.

As He prays, we see a group of soldiers coming over the hill with torches. They come up to Him, and Judas betrays Him with a kiss. The soldiers roughly take the Lord and carry Him before the depraved Herod. There He is laughed at and scorned. Later, He is before the weak Pilate. His back is bared and before the howling mob He is lashed. Imagine anyone striking Christ!

Without even a trial, He is condemned to death and forced to carry a very heavy cross toward Calvary. The shouting mob lines the street. The cross is so heavy and He is in such a weakened condition that He faints under the load. A man has to help carry the cross, and they finally get to the top of the hill.

He is laid on the cross and nails are driven through His hands and feet. The cross is set in place. The soldiers gamble for His clothes, laugh at and mock Him. The physical agony is terrible, yet it isn't nearly so bad as the mental agony, the humiliation, and the bitter disappointment.

You see His lips moving. He is talking to God. You move closer and hear Him saying, "Father, forgive them."

I told this woman who said she could not forgive to keep those pictures on the screen of her mind while we looked briefly at another picture. "You," I said, "are the central character in this picture, and you are before the throne of God for your own judgment."

There all our past sins are brought before us. The idle words, the wrong deeds, the neglected opportunities, and even the wrong thoughts that have been in one's heart.

But you hear a voice saying, "If ye forgive men their trespasses, your heavenly Father will also forgive you: but if ye forgive not men their trespasses, neither will your Father forgive your trespasses" (MATTHEW 6:14-15).

Now, with the picture of Christ on the cross and also the picture of ourselves before the judgment bar of God, I asked the woman how she felt. Before she was harsh, but now she gently whispered, "I can forgive now." She did, and she left with a new song in her heart.

The loving forgiveness of God is what makes life bearable. In the lives of most of us there is a shameful chapter. We can take the way of Judas or the way of Simon Peter. Both sinned, and neither could bear his sin. Judas went out and hanged himself, but Peter came back to Christ.

Our forgiveness of others is not a condition of God's forgiveness of us. Rather it is a condition of our ability to receive the forgiveness of God. We are told by Shakespeare, "The quality of mercy is not strain'd, it droppeth as the gentle rain from heaven." But I could cover a plant with a sheet of iron and the rain could not get to it. So, I can surround my soul with an unforgiving spirit and completely block the forgiving mercy of God.

LEARNING TO FORGIVE

Jesus taught us to pray, "Forgive us our sins, as we forgive those who sin against us." He further said, "If ye forgive men their trespasses, your heavenly Father will also forgive you" (MATTHEW 6:12-14). That is both a glorious promise and an awful warning. To forgive every person, excepting none, is just about the hardest thing we are called on to do. Yet unless we forgive, we cannot be forgiven.

The main reason most of us do not forgive is simply because we do not want to. Before you realize it, bitterness against some other person will spread over your system like a fast growing cancer. It will make you sour and irritable. You develop a martyr-complex, and you begin to pity yourself. Before long you even begin to enjoy your misery. And gradually you become the most helpless creature on earth. To cure a body afflicted with, for example, cancer, is far easier than to take out of one's soul an unforgiving spirit.

I have two suggestions that will succeed whenever they are sincerely tried. Take a sheet of paper and across the top write "The Sins of My Life." Sit down quietly and write down everything you can remember that you have done wrong. Forget about that other person until you finish making your own list. When you have written down all the wrongs and faults of your life you can remember, put the paper aside but keep thinking and as additional things come to mind, add them to the list.

It will be a painful experience. In fact, it will give you a taste of what hell is like. Speaking of hell, Paterson Smyth wrote

> And the ghosts of forgotten actions
> Came floating before my sight,
> And the things that I thought were dead things,
> Were alive with a terrible might.

And the vision of all my past life,
Was an awful thing to face
Alone, alone with my conscience,
In that strange and terrible place.

When you finish your list, then take another sheet of paper and put down whatever it is you do not want to or feel you cannot forgive in that other person. Then compare the two lists. You will see immediately the point in the story Jesus told of the man who was forgiven a debt of two million dollars yet refused to forgive another of only twenty dollars. You will be so ashamed and you will feel so acutely your own need that you will fall on your knees praying, "God be merciful to me a sinner."

But then you will hear our Lord saying, "But if ye forgive not men their trespasses, neither will your Father forgive you" (MATTHEW 6:15). And as you think of your own need of God's forgiveness, you will find it easy to forgive every person you hold anything against. Lord Herbert once said, "He who will not forgive another has broken the bridge over which he himself must pass."

MAGNIFICENT PEOPLE

Sometime ago a man and his wife came to see me. He had done her a terrible wrong. The wife told me the story and asked what she should do. I said, "I think you ought to shoot him. Have you got a gun?" The husband turned a little pale and said, "She's got two guns."

But then I told her that anybody can return evil for evil, get mad, and fly off the handle. Anybody can feel hurt, pout, carry a grudge, and spoil his own life. But some people have what it takes to rise above some things and become magnificent people.

We talked for a while about the forgiveness of God and the forgiveness of each other. She felt that she could not forgive, but she promised to try. We had a prayer together and they left.

Later, when they came back, they did not need to tell me. I could see in their faces that something wonderful had happened. She said, "It is a miracle, but I have been able to forgive." I stood in the door and watched them leave, knowing that she had become a magnificent person. And he, too, because it takes about as much grace to receive forgiveness as it does to forgive.

The most expensive thing you can do is hold a wrong spirit in your heart against another. The price you pay is the loss, the eternal loss, of your own soul.

HOUR OF DESTINY

It is not the work we do, but the spirit within us that determines our real lives. If work is done in the spirit of consecration, it is just as sacred to sell soap as it is to preach sermons, or to be a butcher as it is to be a bishop. Your present work can be done for the glory of God—but there is something more to be said.

For every person who is faithful to the living of each day, there will come an hour of destiny—a time of self-fulfillment. It will come, I emphasize, if we remain faithful to the daily tasks without losing heart or hope. No member of God's team trains for the race without one day being given a chance to run. Sooner or later God says to every person who is ready, "Now—now your moment has come."

EXPRESSING THE EXPERIENCE

After the great transfiguration experience of Christ and some of His disciples on the mountain, we read, "They came down from the mountain" (MATTHEW 8:1). Simon Peter was so thrilled by the spiritual experience on the mountain that he wanted just to stay there. But Christ could see the entire experience. The receiving of the spiritual power was only one side. The expression of that power was the other side. Before any experience is complete it must have expression.

Many people seek the beauty and inspiration of religious faith, but so often they fail to relate it to the tragic need and suffering about them. When we say a person is "going downhill," we think of it in a bad sense.

But from every mountain-top spiritual experience, Christ always came "downhill." As Sidney Lanier expressed it in "The Song of the Chattahoochee":

> Downward the voices of Duty call—
> Downward, to toil and be mixed with the main,
> The dry fields burn, and the mills are to turn,
> And a myriad flowers mortally yearn.

Christ ascended the mountain of prayer; He came down into the valley of service.

AN UNEXPLAINABLE MYSTERY

Recently I flew down the Mississippi for about a hundred miles. It was a beautiful moonlight night, and the great river below our plane looked like a flowing silver ribbon as the soft beams of the moon played on it.

It gave me a tremendous thrill to watch the river, the greatest in the world. For centuries it has been giving all that it has. It freely pours all of its water into the big Gulf of Mexico.

But suppose the Mississippi decided it could not afford to give so freely, that, instead, it began to hold back for fear it would run dry. Then it would cease to be a river and become a swamp. As a swamp it would be an ugly thing and a breeder of evil.

It gives all it has, but it has not run dry. God takes care of the river. He causes the sun to draw the water out of the gulf into clouds, the winds carry the clouds back up the river, and the clouds pour the water back. What the river gives, it gets back.

One of the unexplainable but true mysteries of life is that you never lose what you give. The wisest man who ever walked on this earth said, "He that loseth his life for my sake shall find it" (MATTHEW 10:39). No person ever really begins to live until he finds something big enough to give himself to.

Service without power gained through worship is inadequate, but worship which does not express itself in service is worthless.

LOSING ONE'S LIFE

Often God makes known His will to us through the direct workings of providence. Look at the life of Dr. Albert Schweitzer, considered by many one of the great Christians of all time. He was trying to settle on his life's work. He had so many abilities—for music, for medicine, for teaching—and he was a master in each of those fields. There were uncounted opportunities for him. What should he do? What was God's plan for him?

One day he was cleaning off his desk. Among the papers there was a little magazine of the Paris Missionary Society. It was addressed to a neighbor but by mistake had been put in his mailbox. He glanced through it and noticed an article entitled, "The Needs of the Congo Mission." He read the article and when he finished, Dr. Schweitzer said, "My search is over." To the Congo he went and there he lived one of the greatest lives any of us can imagine.

Let me ask you, was it just an accident that the postman put that little magazine in the wrong mailbox? Was it mere chance that it lay there for days unnoticed until just that moment when Dr. Schweitzer's mind was open to receive direction? No, we believe the hand of God was moving upon the life of that man. It is as the hymn-writer said, "God moves in a mysterious way."

There is something else to be seen in that experience. Dr. Schweitzer might have said, "I have too much to bury it in the far-away Congo." But he didn't say that. He was willing to lose himself in God's plan and it was as Jesus said it would be, ". . . he that loseth his life for my sake shall find it" (MATTHEW 10:39).

When Christ comes into the heart and soul of a man, then that man becomes a part of all other men. Every man then becomes his neighbor.

LIVE AND HELP LIVE

To live and let live is only half the meaning of "thou shalt not kill." Positively, it means to live and help live. Jesus did not find it necessary to warn us against becoming gangsters and murderers, but very clearly does He condemn those who pass by on the other side of a wounded brother. The very foundation of this commandment is the fact that God values every man as He values me. One God who hath made of one blood all nations. One God who is the Father and all men who are brothers. The rule of living means that we look at all men in the proper light.

BURDENS

Notice these three statements from the Bible—they seem contradictory: "For every man shall bear his own burden" (GALATIANS 6:5); "Bear ye one another's burdens . . ." (GALATIANS 6:2); "Cast thy burden upon the Lord . . ." (PSALM 55:22). But when you study the words which are translated "burden," you see they have different meanings. The "burdens" which we are to bear are our rightful obligations of life. The "burdens" of others which we are to bear are those extra burdens which are too heavy for one person, those unexpected troubles. But the "burdens" which we are to cast upon the Lord refer to those which are beyond human hands and help.

The evil and wrong in our world will never be destroyed or driven out until good people are aroused enough to do something about it. Truly, there are times to become righteously indignant.

Once a pen remarked, "I am writing the book." But the ink replied, "I am writing a book. You could not make a mark if it were not for me." The paper replied, "But what could either of you do without me?" Then the dictionary said, "If I did not supply the words no book could be written." And all during the argument the author just smiled.

HEAVENLY TREASURES

We "lay up treasures in heaven" as we live for God, as we invest in deeds of love, in acts of forgiveness and understanding. We become rich toward God as we turn our backs on deeds that are wrong and shoddy and cheap; and as we take our place in the service of life, we make deposits in the bank of heaven when we live with hope, courage, faith, and love; and as we trust God with the explanations which we cannot now understand. When we live in loyal obedience to Christ, we accumulate wealth that will outlast this earth. The Bible teaches us that even a cup of water given in His name will draw rich dividends.

MONEY AND THE GOSPEL

Jesus had more to say about money than any other subject. He began His preaching by saying, "Repent ye," and throughout His ministry He emphasized the necessity of repentance. Yet He talked about money more than He did repentance. He talked to people about forgiveness, about happiness, about eternal life. He emphasized the power of faith and the strength of love. Yet He talked more about money than any of these things. One third of all His parables and one sixth of all the verses in the four Gospels are about money.

Why did He talk so much about money? Certainly He did not try to get money for Himself. I do not recall a single instance of Him taking a collection. As far as we know His only possession was the cloak which He wore. He wanted to capture the souls of men for God, and He knew that money was His chief rival. "You cannot serve God and mammon," He said (LUKE 16:13).

He wanted people to serve God with the same intelligence and enthusiasm with which they served money. People will get up early every morning, hurry to a job and work all day in order to get money. Some people will take all the money they have and use it to build a factory or a store or some other business in order to get more money. Some people will steal, lie, even murder, to get money. Never one time did Jesus condemn money. He never said it was wrong to earn money.

The trouble with money is it can make us so shortsighted. We can forget there is anything else to life, and we can make the ministering to our physical needs and desires the main goal of our lives. Therein lies the danger of money. And when money becomes our God, we always end up disappointed. Judas let money blind him to the things of life that really counted. He got money and then realized what a sorry bargain he had made. He cast his money away and went out and hanged himself. The one who gives his life to material things eventually discovers that neither the things nor the life are worth having.

6

Here's a Faith For You

Faith is like a boomerang: begin using what you have and it comes back to you in greater measure.

A THREEFOLD CONFIDENCE

James M. Barrie wrote: "The reason birds can fly and we can't is simply that they have perfect faith, for to have faith is to have wings." That is, if we have the faith, we will somehow get the means to carry out that faith. The Wright brothers did have faith that men could fly, and they developed the wings. When we ask God and when we ask with faith, immediately we rid our minds of our destructive failure thoughts and we begin to develop a marvelous confidence—a threefold confidence.

1. We develop confidence in ourselves. A man who has lost his nerve is a pitiful creature. He shrinks from every task and he turns away from every opportunity. But when he believes in himself, he develops power and strength he did not know he had.

But on the other hand, we must remind ourselves that confidence in ourselves is not enough. It is good as far as it goes but it doesn't go far enough. We like to quote William E. Henley's poem, "Invictus," in which he talks about his "unconquerable soul," how under adverse circumstance he has not "winced or cried aloud" and how triumphantly he says, "I am the master of my fate, I am the captain of my soul." But in the end Henley committed suicide. He made a good try, but self-confidence was not enough.

2. Also, when we believe, we develop faith in our friends. "No man liveth unto himself"—we need the support of each other. Why do men and women marry? It isn't just the physical relationship. Human beings have needs deeper than physical needs and true faith leads us to believe in the goodness and reliability of other people, and to draw strength from our friendships. But we have needs that human resources cannot supply. And so:

3. True faith not only leads us to self-confidence and confidence in other people, it also leads us to have confidence in God. The Bible says, "But without faith it is impossible to please him: for he that cometh to God must believe that he is, and that he is a rewarder of them that diligently seek him" (HEBREWS 11:6). So for the person of faith, the philosophy of life, "Try asking God," has great meaning.

Faith takes up where sight leaves off. The Bible says, "Now faith is . . . the evidence of things not seen" (HEBREWS 11:1). Faith pierces the darkness of our hearts and knows there is an answer, a reason— a good reason—and it accepts that fact and keeps moving toward God.

BLUEPRINT FOR BELIEVING

Believing is drawing a mental blueprint and, when you accomplish that, the word "impossible" is eliminated from your thinking. When you see it clearly in your mind, it may not yet be actual but you will know it is possible. To help in the process of believing, I suggest three preliminary steps:

1. Write it down. You will find this difficult to do but keep working at it. Before an architect decides on the final drawings of a house, he makes many sketches and as he goes along he erases and redraws many lines.

2. After you have what you really want written, read it over several times each day, making such additions and changes as you desire. When you have it clearly stated, then reduce what you have written to not more than fifty words.

3. Consider your own resources and ask yourself what price you are willing to pay to have your prayer answered. Often it is that God has already answered our prayers. By that I mean, He has already given us the resources, and it only remains for us to apply those resources properly. But sometimes we don't really want our prayers answered because the price we must pay, we feel, is too high. God sometimes answers our prayers independently of us, but usually He answers through us.

The Gospel does not tell us to "try harder." What it does tell us to do is, "Believe harder." There is tremendous strength in belief in Christ.

When you stand in the strength of Christ, don't think about the possibility of falling. We remember how Peter walked on the water as long as he kept looking at Christ. When he began to look at the winds and waves, he began to sink.

KEEPING THE FAITH

Practice keeping faith day by day, and one day you will have enough to keep you.

There are three thoughts to keep in mind, which will help us to keep our faith. The first is: when tempted to give up or lose faith, look back and remember the times you won the victory. Maybe it was some crisis fifteen years ago. You did not see how you could go on, but you did go on and it worked out all right. You discovered new courage and strength inside you that you did not know you had.

Later some other crisis came into your life. You did not see a chance for yourself, but you kept holding on. Maybe some friends helped you that you had not counted on. Anyway, you got through it. Sometime later, still another crisis developed. You can't explain it, but as you kept walking through the dark, suddenly you came out into the sunshine. It seemed to work out providentially. As you look back now, you decide it *was* providential. We do have unused resources; there are friends who help; God does take a hand in our lives. And somehow we eventually come to believe that no matter what life does to us, we can go on. That belief helps us to keep the faith. A second help in keeping the faith is not to forget that, though life has a way of pulling us down, there are even stronger forces in life that holds us up. Life may hurt us, but even more it aids us.

Life has the power to hurt, to hurt deeply; but life also has the power to heal, to heal completely. When you are tempted to give up your faith, remember that life's helping power is stronger than its hurting power.

A third fact to remember when you are tempted not to keep faith is to remember some of the great triumphs faith has won for others, and also remember you are made of the same stuff of which they were made.

Fix in your mind, for example, Mozart. When he was twenty-five, he went to Vienna. There, ten years later, he died. During those ten years he wrote his matchless music, which will live forever. One day his publisher said to him harshly, "Write, sir, in a more easy and popular style; or I will neither print your music nor pay you a penny for it."

Mozart and his wife were so poor that they often had neither food nor fuel in their tiny house. One cold morning that winter, a friend who came to visit Mozart found his house entirely without heat and the composer and his wife waltzing to keep warm. In fact, the cold and hunger put him in his grave when he was thirty-five.

It must have been an almost unbearable temptation to him to sacrifice his standards. He might so easily have said, "After all, a man has to eat." Or even more easily said, "I cannot see my wife suffer." Instead, he said to his publisher, "Then, my good sir, I have only to resign and die of starvation. I cannot write as you demand." And starve he did; but isn't the world proud of him? The faith he kept is still keeping him.

And when you are tempted not to keep your faith, it will help you to remember that within you is something of what was in Mozart. There is something within every person which, if given a chance, will make that person invincible. That something is God, for God is in us.

Faith makes its plea and then leaves the how and the when of the answer in God's hand.

BORN BELIEVING

God does not depend on reasons or arguments for our belief in Him. God took care of that in our creation. Call it instinct, insight, intuition, or any other name, we were born believing. As we study and learn, as we live and experience, our belief can be strengthened and enlarged. Or our belief can be perverted and misdirected. Therein lies the danger. The Ten Commandments do not command us to believe, but they do command us to keep God as the first object of our worship.

The first cause of failure is lack of faith. Failure and faith are incompatible words—they simply cannot exist together. If you have faith, you will not fail; if you fail, it is a sign that you do not have faith. Faith may have setbacks, but faith never knows failure.

The struggle in prayer is the struggle to believe. And what is it to believe? It means to see your desire as an accomplished fact in your mind. You must be able to visualize it though it has not actually come to pass. That is one important type of believing.

CONVERT YOUR FEARS

The worst enemy of your life is perverted fear. I say perverted because basically fear is good. God made man with the capacity to be afraid for man's own protection. Only a fool is fearless. Because a student fears an examination, he prepares for it. We read, "The fear of the Lord is the beginning of knowledge" (PROVERBS 1:7). Fear develops humility, reverence, and faith.

But when fear is perverted it becomes a monster which paralyzes and destroys one's life. We remember the story Jesus told of the man who buried his talent in the ground. "I was afraid," he said. His talent was taken away from him, and he was called an unprofitable servant (MATTHEW 25:25-30). And today there are vast numbers of people whose lives are "unprofitable" simply because they are paralyzed by fear.

GOD-GIVEN FAITH

When a baby is born, God gives it faith just the same as He gives it hands and feet. A child needs to learn to walk, but it is born with the capacity to walk. The teacher cannot give a child intelligence; the teacher teaches the child to use its intelligence. The child cannot be given music; the teacher teaches the child to express the music it possesses.

As energy cannot be created or destroyed, neither can faith be. But faith can lie unused within us. It can be covered up and not used.

USING THE FAITH WE HAVE

How can I get faith? Where can I find it? You don't get faith—you already have it. The only place you can find it is within yourself. And the only way you can find it is to look for your faith instead of your fears and your failures.

People die, businesses fail, automobiles are wrecked, jobs are lost, homes are broken up, friends are betrayed, lives are ruined. When you fill your mind with that sort of thing, no wonder you lose sight of your faith and think you have lost it. But just for one day, keep a list of the times you express faith. You will be surprised.

I step out of bed in the morning onto the floor. I believe the floor will hold me up. I take a drink of water. The water comes from a muddy river contaminated with filth. In many places in the world a person would not dare drink water until it was boiled. But I drink the water believing it has been purified. I eat scrambled eggs for breakfast. My wife could have put arsenic in the eggs, but I have faith that she didn't.

I stop at the filling station for ten gallons of gasoline. I don't have a can to measure the gas—I have faith that I'll get what I pay for. I stop at the mailbox to mail a payment on my life insurance. I am depending on that insurance to mean a lot to my wife and children if I should die, to help me if I should get sick, to be a friend to me if I should be unable to work when I am old. That insurance means a lot to me, yet I mail the payments to an office I have never seen, to be handled by people I will never know. I have faith that they will do what they say. Space doesn't permit the naming of the many times I use faith in one day.

So it is in life. We automatically use faith in a thousand different ways; but sometimes when we come to a place when we must consciously use faith, we shrink back. Instead of thinking of your loads to lift, think of your own abilities, the support of other people, and especially the help of God. And as you think of your power instead of your problems, you will find that faith comes easily and naturally. And you will not then be afraid of failure.

GROWTH OF THE MUSTARD SEED

Jesus said, "If ye have faith as a grain of mustard seed, ye shall say unto this mountain, Remove hence to yonder place; and it shall remove, and nothing shall be impossible unto you" (Matthew 17:20).

Many of us misread that verse. We think of a grain of mustard seed as a little thing and conclude that Jesus was saying, If ye have only a little faith. A grain of sand is also little, but Jesus did not say as a grain of sand.

The difference is that a grain of sand is a dead, fixed thing, while a grain of mustard seed is a live thing with capacity for growth and development.

What Jesus was saying is that if we will take what faith we have, even though it seems small and insignificant, and begin to use it, we will accomplish things that before seemed impossible.

It does not mean that suddenly you will accomplish everything overnight. The mustard seed does not grow that way. Instead, the seed is planted in the ground. As it grows it draws food and warmth from the earth. Even though it is buried in the ground, it realizes there is sunshine above and it begins to push up.

The mustard seed is not discouraged because it is little. Instead, it pictures itself as a large plant, and it is never satisfied until it reaches its fullest possible maturity.

And Jesus is telling you that, instead of worrying about how little you have or how meager your opportunities are, if you will take what you have and begin to use it, drawing on every possible resource as you go, never quitting, you will grow bigger than the mountain of any problem in your life.

There are many who sincerely want to believe in God but find it hard. Faith never comes easy, and the only way it can come is by beginning where we can begin and going on from there. No one believes in all of God. No one can. God is so great and we are so small that we can only believe in a part of Him. A man once said to Jesus, "Lord, I believe; help thou mine unbelief" (MARK 9:24). And in every person there is both belief and unbelief. No person believes completely.

IS YOUR GOD TOO SMALL?

The trouble with a lot of people is: their God is too small. St. Paul said, ". . . My God shall supply all your need . . ." (PHILIPPIANS 4:19). In that statement he reveals that his God is a big God. But when you say, "My God," what do you mean?

I know of a man in New York who died recently at the age of seventy. As a young man of twenty, he married and opened a little shop on a side street. He and his wife lived in a tiny apartment on the East Side. Six mornings a week he would get up, eat his breakfast, walk to the subway station and ride to his work. All day long he spent in his shop. Because he never had another clerk, he carried his lunch from home and ate on the job.

At closing time he would catch the subway back, eat his supper, and soon go to bed. He was never a strong man so he rested in bed every Sunday. For fifty years that was his routine, and then he died. When that man said, "My city," he meant a tiny apartment, a subway train, and a shop on a side street. He never saw the Metropolitian Museum, or rode to the top of the Empire State Building, or mingled with the crowds on Fifth Avenue. "My city" was for him a very limited experience.

When you say "My God," what do you mean? For St. Paul, "My God" meant one great enough to cover his entire life—". . . shall supply all your need," he said. Unless your God is that big, then He is too small.

No person believes perfectly; neither does any person doubt completely. Within every one of us is both belief and doubt. The question is, which do we hold before us? If you will begin by emphasizing your belief, by practicing what faith you have, it will grow. You believe something about God; what is it? That is the place for you to begin.

THE BIBLE IN MINIATURE

What is the Christian faith? Thousands of sermons are preached every day explaining it, and many books have been written on what a Christian believes, but the best answer has been given in just twenty-five words:

"For God so loved the world, that he gave his only begotten Son, that whosoever believeth in him should not perish, but have everlasting life" (JOHN 3:16).

Martin Luther called that verse "the Bible in miniature," because it so completely sums up the Christian Gospel.

1. It gives us a definition of God. There have been many words used to define God. "Holy" is the word of the Old Testament. Rome chose the word "power." Greece took the word "wisdom." Paganism used the word "mystery." Modern science uses the word "energy."

We might name a hundred words, each of which would define some part of God. None would be entirely wrong but each word would be inadequate. But here Jesus gives us the word "love," which is the word that most completely describes God.

2. Then, here is the definition of love—"God so loved . . . that he gave . . . ." Here love is not sentiment but service, not emotion but action.

This is a revolutionary idea of God. Previously, religions had presented God as a receiving God. They built altars of sacrifice, on which they placed their finest lambs and first fruits. Religion became a burden.

To many people today religion is only a burden. We are expected to give much merely in return for a dim promise of some distant eternal reward.

But Christianity teaches that true religion is not bringing our gifts to God, but rather God coming out of His invisibility to pour His treasures at our feet.

3. What did God give? It is so easy to think of God giving laws that bind and restrict us. Many think of Him as a giant Santa Claus giving material things.

Emerson wrote a wonderful essay on "Gifts" in which he said, "Rings and other jewels are not gifts. They are apologies for gifts. The only gift is a portion of thyself."

"He gave his only begotten son"—a portion of Himself.

Robert Browning has a poem entitled "One Word More." It is the story of a man trying to express his love for a woman. He tried poetry, prose, paintings, sculpture, but always he fails and longs for one word more.

Down through the centuries God has sought to reveal Himself in history, literature, prophecy, poetry, and through the lives of men. Then, in the fulness of time, He gave Himself. The love of God was made flesh and then we beheld His glory.

4. Here is a definition of faith: "that whosoever believeth in Him . . ." Faith here is a personal thing. It is not acceptance of some creed; it is belief in a person.

The Christian is not so much concerned about *what* he believes as he is about *whom* he believes. I often get mixed up thinking about what to believe, but I get straightened out again when I start thinking about Him.

5. Finally, here is the definition of salvation: "whosoever believeth in him should not perish, but have everlasting life."

The word perish here is the same word as is used when the Prodigal Son said, "I perish with hunger." We understand what that means.

To believe in Christ and His way of life, to follow His example, to seek to know His will, is to enter into life. Salvation means to live, to live on this side of the grave as well as on the other side.

There are five key words: God—love—gave—Himself—life.

7

Walk Through the Portals of Prayer

Prayer is need finding a voice—embarrassment seeking relief—a friend in search of a Friend—knocking on a barred door—reaching out through the darkness. Prayer is speaking, or thinking, or feeling with the belief that there is Somebody who hears and who cares and who will respond. Prayer is a means of contact with God. Prayer is opening our lives to the purposes of God.

SEEKING THE SOURCE

The beginning of prayer is a right relationship with God; without that beginning we merely speak words and call them prayers. Recently a friend of mine gave me a beautiful electric lamp for my desk. Carefully and lovingly he made it for me, and it is a thing of beauty. But suppose I take it home, turn the switch, and no light comes. I might conclude that all electric lamps are a fake. The trouble may be in the lamp. On the other hand, it may be that I failed to connect it to the source of power. The world is filled with electricity, but until I connect my lamp to it, it will not burn.

So with prayer. I may use the most beautiful words and phrases, but until I am connected with the great Source of power, my prayers are just meaningless words. Jesus said some people ". . . think that they shall be heard for their much speaking. Be not ye therefore like unto them: for your Father knoweth what things ye have need of before ye ask him. After this manner therefore pray ye: Our Father which art in heaven, Hallowed be thy name" (MATTHEW 6:7-9). That is, before you consider the results of prayer, get connected with the Source.

Prayer clears one's vision and helps him to see better what can be done; prayer gives one inspiration to get up and start doing what he can.

ON BEING RECEPTIVE

The beginning of prayer is to receive God. That means we must pray in a receptive mood. You get up in the morning thinking of the things you must do that day. Your mind is active and aggressive and hour by hour during the day you spend your thought, time and effort in your work and activities. Then that night you attend a concert of great music. But to enjoy the concert, you must change your mood. Instead of being aggressively active, at the concert you must become receptive. Likewise, when we pray, we must be receptive.

SEVEN SIMPLE STEPS

The disciples once said to Christ, "Lord, teach us to pray." It is the only thing they ever asked Him to teach them. They knew that, once they learned to pray, the power of God was at their disposal.

In response to that request, Christ gave them seven simple steps to follow. He needed only sixty-six words (MATTHEW 6:9-13), and the power is available to any who follow those steps.

1. Start by thinking of God. Forget about your own needs and problems for the time being and saturate your mind with thoughts of God. This will silence the mind and bring relaxation. Think of Him as "Our Father which art in heaven." You cannot imagine a cyclone in heaven. Heaven suggests calmness, beauty, and rest. Note the first word is "Our." You cannot pray for yourself alone.

2. Then let your prayer begin with thanking God for what He has done for you. Think of some definite blessings you have received and "name them one by one." You cannot hope to name them all, but do name some. This leads to positive and constructive thinking. It tends to diminish our bitterness, disappointment, and defeatist attitudes. "Hallowed be Thy name."

3. Naturally, the next step is consecration—"Thy kingdom come, thy will be done." As we think of the benefits we have received from God, we want Him more and more in our lives and in our world. We realize that it is better for us to have God, and we increasingly want Him to have full possession of us. Possessing us, we want to help Him possess the world about us.

So we pray that God will use us in His work. We begin to see things we might do to help, and we gladly commit ourself to those opportunities. Anything that we can do to bring His Kingdom in we eagerly become willing to do.

4. As you realize the greatness of God, you understand that all we have comes from His hand, that if God stopped giving for even one minute, every bit of life on earth would cease. We think of our complete dependence on Him. So we pray, "Give us this day our daily bread."

Back of the loaf is the snowy flour, and back of the flour
    is the mill;
And back of the mill is the sheaf, and the shower and
    the sun, and the Father's will.

5. Then, when we realize that wrong within our own lives blocks out our ability to serve, and also feeling our utter dependence on God, confession comes next. "Forgive us our sins" is the fifth step.

Here we need to be specific. In dealing with many people, I have come to see that it is usually some definite wrong that needs to be settled. When we become willing to turn loose "that one thing," we usually have little difficulty in settling all the other things that are wrong.

6. As we seek forgiveness of our own sins we are simultaneously seeking the forgiveness of every other person. Because as God comes into our own hearts, there also comes in a deep and abiding love for Him and for all other people.

Here we feel the "expulsive power of a new affection." Prejudice, jealousy, hate, grudges, and indifference cannot live in a heart into which God has come. Thus it is easy and natural to pray, "As we forgive others."

7. Finally comes the most important step of all. It is "Amen." That is a big and strong word. Literally, it means, "So let it be." It is a resolve of honesty. Obviously it would be dishonest and unfair to ask God to do for us what we are unwilling to do for ourselves. That word "Amen" is a promise that you will do all within your own power to answer your prayer.

Also, "Amen" means what Jesus meant when He said, "Into thy hands I commend my spirit" (LUKE 23:46). That is, I have done my best and now I am willing to leave the results to God. It is a pledge of faith and confidence. Thus, when one has prayed, his mind can be at rest in the assurance that God has heard and will answer.

Those seven simple steps are the "how" of prayer and, when honestly taken, they become the pathway to power—power that gives light and understanding, a clean heart, and harmony within the soul.

The result of our prayer is not what we may have persuaded God to do, but rather what God can work in us to the accomplishment of our highest purposes and greatest needs and desires.

Prayer is not a method of using God; rather is prayer a means of reporting for duty to God.

PREPARATION FOR PRAYER

In prayer, it often happens that one just rambles around in his praying, with no definite purpose or object. I have suggested to many people that in preparation for prayer they should write down exactly why they are praying and the answers they are seeking. One may write for several pages, but after he has written his thoughts, he should reduce what he has written to about fifty words.

Sometime ago, I wrote a letter, which was a full page long, to a person. After I finished the letter I realized it would not reach the person in time, so instead I sent a telegram. I reduced the thought of that page-long letter into a fifteen-word telegram, and, really, I think I said it more clearly in the fifteen words than in the entire page! So, reduce your thinking to about fifty words until they are clear in your mind. It is amazing how much clearer and easier praying becomes when we eliminate from our prayers our "repetitions" and our "much speaking."

Let us remember that Jesus gave us the Lord's Prayer, which has become a model for all Christian prayer, and it contains only sixty-six words.

DIVINE PROVISION

It is good for me to pray about the salvation of my soul. It is just as much in order for me to ask God to help me get a job or to bless my business. And the God who made bluebirds and violets surely wants us to have not only the bare necessities, but also some of the lovely luxuries. Not only is He anxious for us to have bread, but also He is glad when we have some cake.

INGREDIENTS OF PRAYER

In his *Paradiso*, Dante says that Peter represents faith; James, hope; and John, love. Whether there is actual Scriptural basis for that or not, the fact is that those qualities are the essential ingredients of prayer: faith that the answer is possible; hope that causes us to concentrate on the solutions rather than on the problems; love that rids our lives of selfishness, of jealousy and envy, that teaches us the meaning of sacrificial living.

MEETING THE CONDITIONS

God wants to give us many things, but we refuse to meet the conditions. Here is a room that is dark. It may be that the sun is not shining. It could be that the sun is shining but the windows are so dirty that the light cannot pass through. There are three steps in prayer—asking, giving, and receiving. The psalmist prayed: "Search me, O God, and know my heart; try me, and know my thoughts" (PSALM 139:23). We ourselves must be right with God in order to be able to receive His answers.

Until we feel our prayers with our hearts as well as our minds, they are not real. We cannot approach God on flippant feet. Prayer is not for triflers.

WHATSOEVER

"Whatsoever ye shall ask in my name, that will I do. . ." (JOHN 14:13). In explanation, we must remember four facts:
1. Frequently God has already put within our reach the "whatsoever." There was a boy who asked God to give him a good mark on his examination the next day. He prayed earnestly but he failed the exam. He lost

his faith and bitterly said the promises of God were no good. The next year he decided he did not need God, he could get along by himself. So he repeated the course, studied hard, and passed the exam. It took that boy some years to realize that God had answered his prayer even before he prayed it. God had given him the mental ability to learn the course and pass the exam, but the first year he had not used God's answer. God has already given us the means to possess many of our "whatsoevers."

2. God is wiser than we, and He has the power to distinguish between what we really want and what we think we want at the moment. One summer I rode with the junkman every day. He had a fine horse and I had great fun driving. When September came I told my father I always wanted to work with the junkman and did not want to go back to school. Suppose my father had said, "All right, since you have decided what you want, you may have it"? Being wiser, he could distinguish between my immediate whims and the real desires of my heart. He refused my want but, as Tagore said, "Thou didst save me by Thy hard refusals." Fortunately for us, God answers our larger prayers even though it may require some refusals along the way.

3. God is concerned with all His children and if my "whatsoever" conflicts with someone else's prayer, then with infinite love and wisdom, God answers the prayer that should be answered. Some time back I phoned for a plane reservation and they told me there was no chance. I prayed about it and the next day they phoned to say they had a place for me. Later I was in Dallas, Texas. I could not get a reservation back but I went on out to the airport, confidently believing I would get a seat. I sincerely asked God to help me. But the plane took off without me. I know God could have managed to get someone off that plane, but in that case, it would not have been fair.

4. Remember these lines from our national anthem: "Then conquer we must, when our cause it is just; And this be our motto: 'In God is our trust!'" It may be, and often is, that our "whatsoever" is not just; so, include always in prayer our Lord's words: "Nevertheless not my will, but thine, be done" (LUKE 22:42).

THE HEIGHTS OF PRAYER

Prayer is fellowship with God. Prayer is seeking to understand one's own self. Truly the heights of spiritual experience have been reached by many a man through an honest facing of his true self. Prayer is self-discipline which comes as a result of discovering God's will and then making the necessary adjustments within one's thoughts, feelings, and acts. One of the heights in prayer comes as a result of the mingling of human desire and God's desire. Certainly prayer is in my every relationship with every other person; it is in all my ambitions, in all my activities —it is in all my life.

OCCASIONS FOR PRAYER

It has now become a habit with me to pray every time I see a funeral procession. Even though I do not know who it is, I know that in the cars behind that hearse are some saddened hearts that especially need help. It is not hard for me to pray, "Father, may just now that family especially feel the presence of the sympathizing Jesus."

I always pray when I pass a church building. No matter what denomination it is, people meet in that place to worship God and to gain inspiration for Christian service. Some people stand off and criticize the church, but I know that my community is better because that church is there, so it comes naturally to me to pray for it.

When I see one in the uniform of our country, I am led to say a prayer. On some battlefield that boy or girl may lose his or her life defending me and all I hold dear. I think of the mother and father whose hearts are anxious. Maybe there are a young wife and some little children back home. Prayer for one in service comes very quickly to me. I especially pray that away from home that boy might above all things hold high his standards.

Of course, I always pray for the sick. I pray that God might direct the mind and guide the hand of the physician. I ask a special blessing on the nurse who has such a difficult job yet one so very important. And I pray that the Great Physician might have a definite part in the case.

PRAYING FOR OTHERS

Let me put down for you my own method of praying for another person:

First, pray definitely for that one person. Get that person clearly in your mind so that you can see him or her vividly. Decide as definitely as you can the need of that person, considering the circumstances of his or her life.

Second, holding that particular person in mind, think of God. It helps me to think of some particular scene in the life of Christ that may apply to this situation. For example, if the person has physical needs, think of Christ feeding the five thousand; if the person is living wrong, think of Him saying to that fallen one, "Go and sin no more"; if the person is sick, think of the woman who touched the hem of His garment. Now, you are thinking of God and the particular person together.

Third, think of your prayer as lifting that person into the presence of God. You are not trying to tell God something He does not know. Neither are you trying to persuade God to do something He doesn't want to do. Realize, as Augustine said, "Without God, we cannot; without us, God will not." Think of yourself as supplying the human cooperation that is necessary to bring the person and God together.

Fourth, tell God what is on your heart. Remember, however, to pray positively. Don't concentrate on the person's weakness, sickness, or wrong. Rather, concentrate on the person's strengths and picture in your mind the answer you want and picture that person receiving that answer. Thus, you pray hopefully.

Fifth, keep praying until God's answer comes.

When it comes to prayer, we all stand on equal ground and each has the right of access to the Father. The learned and the unlearned, the rich and the poor, the saint and the sinner, all stand in need before God; and when in prayer they carry that need to God, He answers. Jesus said, "For every one that asketh receiveth . . ." (MATTHEW 7:8), and when He said "every one," He meant just that.

PRAYER SUGGESTIONS

To make the most of prayer, let me suggest nine prayer steps.

There are three steps to take *before* prayer:

1. Decide what you really want. Get clearly in mind exactly what you plan to ask in prayer.

2. Seek to determine whether or not what you want is right. Ask yourself such questions as: Is it fair to everyone else concerned? Is it best for me? Is it in harmony with the Spirit of God?

3. Write it down. Reducing our requests to writing helps to clarify our thinking and deepen the impressions upon our mind and heart.

Then, there are three steps to take *during* prayer:

1. Keep the mind still. Just as the moon cannot be perfectly reflected on a restless sea, so God cannot be experienced by an unquiet mind. "Be still, and know that I am God" (PSALM 46:10). At this point we must concentrate to keep the mind from wandering. There are some books I cannot read while in a comfortable chair, and there are some prayers I cannot pray without being completely at attention. This is what Jesus meant when He said, ". . . when thou hast shut thy door . . ." (MATTHEW 6:6); that is, shut out distracting thoughts.

2. Talk *with* God, and not *to* God. Instead of saying, with Samuel, "Speak; for thy servant heareth" (I SAMUEL 3:10), we are prone to say, "Listen, Lord, for Thy servant speaketh." Prayer is both speaking and listening.

3. Promise God what you yourself will do to answer your own prayer. God answers prayer, not for you, but with you. Jesus performed many of His miracles by giving the person to be helped something to do. As you pray, search for the things that you yourself can do.

Then, there are three steps to take *after* prayer:

1. Always remember to thank God for answering your prayer. You would not pray in the first place if you did not believe God would answer. Now, confirm that belief by thanking Him for the answer, even though it has not yet come.

2. Be willing to accept whatever God's answer may be, remembering the words of our Lord, ". . . nevertheless not my will, but thine, be done" (LUKE 22:42).

3. Do everything loving that comes to your mind. One of the objects of prayer is to bring the love of God into our hearts; and as we express that love, we make it possible for God to answer our prayers better.

Work is a part of the business of living, and we cannot enter the presence of God on lazy feet. Prayer is never a substitute for work. The "mountain top" experiences, the spiritual heights, are gained partly as a result of work.

UNANSWERED PRAYERS

What is the answer for the problem of unanswered prayer?

The fault may be in us. We remember that Jesus warns us that if we refuse to forgive others, God will not forgive us (MATTHEW 6:15). And the Psalmist says, "If I regard iniquity in my heart, the Lord will not hear me" (66:18). James says, "Ye ask, and receive not because ye ask amiss" (JAMES 4:3).

Because of our own refusal to do ourselves what we ask God to do, because of our refusal to face the sin of our own lives, because of asking for the wrong reasons, we do not get the answer we ask for. The first prayer, and the beginning of every prayer, should be, "Search me, O God, and know my heart: try me and know my thoughts" (PSALM 139:23). God makes the sun to shine, but if the window in our house is dirty, God will not make the sun come through. The darkness in your room may not be a cause for asking God to make the sun shine brighter. Rather it may be a cause for you to wash your windows.

The darkness of your soul, and the littleness which you have received, the confusion in which you live, may not be because God has not answered; it may be because you are unwilling to receive. God has two kinds of gifts for us: first, there are the ones he gives whether we ask for them or not—the sun which shines, the air we breathe, the fertility in the soil. Parents give to their children such things as food, shelter, clothing and watchful care whether the child asks for it or not.

The other kind of gifts are given only if we ask for them. I want my son to have a college education, but I cannot give it to him unless he asks for it and wants it. If I make available for him the money he needs, he must cooperate by opening his mind through study in order to receive the education. Yes, the reason we do not receive the answers to our prayers may be in us.

WHEN GOD SAYS NO

If God says "No" to our prayer, it does not mean we should stop praying. It means that we keep praying until we find the prayer to which He can say "Yes." The supreme object of prayer is not the attainment of some desire, but rather is it to know God. Knowing God, we know His purposes and knowing His purposes, we desire them above our own. And desiring His purposes, it then becomes safe for God to entrust us with His power. But God will not give us His power for unworthy uses.

WHEN IT'S DANGEROUS TO PRAY

The fact that prayer is dangerous never occurs to some. We think of prayer as being about the safest thing we can do—but it isn't. Do you remember singing the hymn: "I'll go where you want me to go, dear Lord, O'er mountain, or plain, or sea"? When we sing those words we usually think of the heroic life of some missionary. But be careful before you promise God you'll go where He wants you go. He might not send you to Africa. Instead, he might send you to apologize to and to forgive a certain person. Or He might send you to some obscure service in the church. Or He might send you to render an unpleasant service to some other person.

It takes a strong man to get on his knees before God.

WHY SOME DON'T PRAY

There are vast numbers who have desperate needs but never really pray. Why? Because they do not actually believe that any real help would come from God. Vast numbers of people are practical atheists. They intellectually believe in the existence of a God, but not to the extent that they count on God to take a hand in the affairs of their own lives. Thus, if we do not believe God can or will help us, we see no need of praying.

MOVING MOUNTAINS

Jesus spoke about how prayer can remove mountains. However, we need to remember there are two ways by which a mountain can cease to block our paths. One way is to move it. The other is to develop the strength to walk over the top of the mountain and keep going. In answer to our prayers, sometimes God takes away our handicaps; at other times He gives us the strength to keep going in spite of what has happened.

CLAIMING THE POWER OF CHRIST

They stood one day on the deck of a ship in the midst of a raging sea. They heard Him say quietly but with authority, "Peace, be still" (MARK 4:39), and they were amazed as the winds and the waves obeyed His voice. He would speak to one paralyzed for many years, and they watched the man get up and walk.

They picked up twelve baskets full of leftovers after a crowd of 5,000 had eaten, yet all He had to begin with was a boy's lunch of five loaves and two fishes. They saw blind people, epileptics, lepers, even mentally deranged, healed with just a word from His lips. They saw the haunting burden of guilt drain out of human faces as He forgave. They heard Him speak as no man ever spoke. They felt the magnetism of His own life.

But their amazing wonder was changed into fearful responsibility when they heard Him say,"As my Father hath sent me, even so send I you" (JOHN 20:21). Surely they could not be expected to work His miracles. It was too much to ask of them. But they were filled with an awe-inspiring sense of possibility as He said to them: "Verily, verily, I say unto you, He that believeth on me, the works that I do shall he do also; and greater works than these shall he do; because I go unto my father" (JOHN 14:12).

Could it be true that such power could be theirs? He said so, thus it was so. But how? Would He teach them His secrets? One day the answer burst upon them. There was one golden key to the powerhouse of God. Eagerly they said, "Lord, teach us to pray" (LUKE 11:1). Learning to pray was the one, the only, secret they needed to know.

In response, Jesus gave them a prayer (MATTHEW 6:9-13). It can be said in one quarter of a minute, just fifteen seconds. Even for a large congregation of people to repeat it slowly takes only half a minute. Yet Jesus would spend half the night praying that same prayer. Today there are millions of people who can say that prayer, but very few ever learn to pray it. The power comes not in the saying, but in the praying of the prayer.

Praying is not saying words. Words merely form the frame on which the temple of thought is built. The power of the Lord's Prayer is not in the words, but rather in the pattern of thinking in which our minds are formed. The Bible tells us, "Be ye transformed by the renewing of your mind" (ROMANS 12:2). When our thoughts begin to flow in the channels of the Lord's Prayer our minds do become new, and we are transformed.

To the extent that we think the thoughts of Christ, to that same extent do we have the power of Christ.

8

Christ Offers You Salvation

Accepting Christ as your Saviour is not some little moral reform; it is a new birth and a new life.

CHRIST AS SAVIOUR

We have a dangerous tendency of thinking of our Lord as a teacher before we think of Him as the Saviour. This can be a fatal mistake. Without our knowing Christ as the Saviour, His teachings can be so beyond our reach that they do not help us, but merely lead us to despair. For example, imagine saying to people with defective lives and vile hearts that they should be "pure in heart." One cannot hope to understand, much less live by, the teachings of our Lord until that one has had the spiritual experience with Him that leads one to know Him as Saviour and Lord and Friend. We become changed by Him rather than by His teaching.

FOOLISHLY BRAVE

Temptation most often comes first as thoughts. In the secret places of our minds we dramatize and act out the thoughts. We read books that describe wickedness; we play with emotional dynamite as if it were a harmless toy. We get ourselves into dangerous situations and enjoy being there. We keep the wrong company. When we go about work or pleasure some enticing voice may whisper, "Brother, lend me your soul." We might hesitate to give away a dime, even if we have a pocketful of coins, but we risk our souls though we know it may be for eternity. When it is temptation we face we are foolishly brave.

Not so with Jesus. He tells us to fear the temptation of the morrow more than any other thing. Our very strength is our greatest weakness, because the overconfidence in our strength leads to our downfall. We are afraid of our weaknesses and guard against them. But we take chances with our strengths, and that is where we lose. "Wherefore let him that thinketh he standeth take heed lest he fall" (I CORINTHIANS 10:12).

One has committed the unpardonable sin when, because of continued indifference to God and continuance of evil habits, he forms a Godless character and becomes incapable of hearing or responding to God's Spirit.

God already knows all about us. Confession is our recognition that what we have done is wrong; it also means our desire to have it taken out of our lives and hearts. We do not need to persuade God to forgive. As we look at the cross we realize that He loves us and goes to the uttermost for us.

BARTIMAEUS AND THE GOSPEL

There are six main steps in the Christian gospel. We see each of them clearly illustrated in the story of Jesus and Bartimaeus. First, there is the need. In this case it was physical blindness. "Blind Bartimaeus sat by the highway side begging," the story says, and immediately our hearts go out to him.

Of all our physical faculties, we probably cherish the ability to see the most. We would rather lose our hearing, or our ability to speak, or even our arms or legs than to lose our sight. To help us to see more we have developed the microscope and the telescope. We have spent millions and millions on motion pictures, and now television is one of our largest industries. We like to see, and we sympathize with one who is blind. I heard of a blind man on the corner with his tin cup that stopped nearly every passerby. About his neck was a sign reading, "It is May and I am blind."

People who have let hate, greed, selfishness or something else blind their hearts are in even greater need. The need might be the burden of a guilty conscience, or the loss of a reason for living, or a broken heart, or some depressing fear or some other need.

Because of that need in our lives that we ourselves cannot meet, we feel that life is passing us by. Bartimaeus was not out in the procession marching with his fellows. He sat by the highway side—he was on the sideline. Maybe he had become afficted with an even worse need in that he had given up and become resigned to his place. He could see no better days ahead—he had grown hopeless. Whatever our need, realizing it is the first step of the Christian gospel.

Second, is the awakening of our belief in Christ and our desire for Him. Doubtless some passerby said to Bartimaeus, "Why don't you get up from the sideline of life and make yourself count for something?" Pitifully he replied, "Don't mock me. You know I would, except I am blind. I cannot do anything."

In my imagination I can hear the man's reply: "There is a man named Jesus, of the house of David. He has been doing marvelous things for people. He caused the daughter of Jairus to live again, he fed five thousand people with one little boy's lunch, he healed ten lepers, he quieted the wild man who lived in the cemetery, he has caused deaf men to hear and even blind men to see."

That is the best news Bartimaeus has ever heard. Hope begins to rise in his heart, a desire to meet this Jesus takes possession of him, and he begins to feel the thrill of a new expectancy.

One day as blind Bartimaeus sits by the highway side, he hears a multitude approaching. Someone calls the name of Jesus, and the blind man's heart begins to leap within him. Jesus, the One who can cause him to see, the One who can meet his need is now nearby. Bartimaeus begins to cry out, "Jesus, thou son of David, have mercy on me."

That is the third step of the Christian gospel—we must ask for Christ's help. Jesus told us, "And all things whatsoever ye shall ask in prayer, believing, ye shall receive" (MATTHEW 21:22). The limit He places is not on His ability or willingness to give, but on our willingness to ask and our capacity to believe. No greater moment comes into the life of any person than when, out of a recognition of need and faith in Christ's power to meet that need, he falls on his knees in humility and begins to pray.

Notice the prayer of this blind man. He prays without apology. There are some people around who try to stop him, but he pays no attention. There are always some to scoff at the power of prayer and there is always danger of being so concerned about what others might think that we miss its blessing. But Bartimaeus is only concerned about his need and the power of Christ to meet that need, and when someone tries to stop him, the Bible says, "he cried the more a great deal."

And what does he pray? He doesn't try to explain that his blindness is no worse than somebody else's. He doesn't try to excuse himself. "Have mercy upon me," he says. That is all, and that was enough. Christ can always tell when one is sincere and when the prayer comes really from the heart.

"And Jesus stood still," we read. That is the fourth step. What a marvelous revelation of God that is! In company with a multitude, Christ was bent on some mission. But above the noise of the crowd He heard the cry for help, and He stopped. Prayer has the power to stop God and center His attention upon you—just you. Suppose this blind man had not prayed? Christ would have passed him by. And how many needs are there in your life that are not met simply because you have not prayed? How many times has God passed you by because you did not ask Him to stop?

This man whose prayer stopped Christ was not the ruler of the country, not some very prominent or influential person; he was a mere beggar. He was a man who was on the very bottom rung of the social ladder. But in the face of the need of just one obscure person, the Son of God stopped and to him gave His full attention and made available His mighty power.

Now notice the fifth step in that story: "And he, casting away his garment, rose, and came to Jesus."

His garment—probably an old coat he had. It was not wrong for him to have it, and no doubt he enjoyed wearing it. But in this instance that coat was a hindrance. By holding on to the coat he could not get to Christ as easily and as quickly. So without hesitation he cast it aside. It is at this point so many fail. We do want Christ, but there are some other things we are unwilling to give up. It may be something that is good, but it takes our time and attention and keeps us away from Him. As long as there is anything which you are not willing to surrender, you cannot possess the power of the Saviour.

Sin and sinful habits is one of the coats we must cast aside. He said, "Blessed are the pure in heart: for they shall see God" (MATTHEW 5:8). Whatever wrong I have done, He stands ready and able to forgive it, but even He cannot forgive until I forsake it. When you kneel to pray, is there something that stands between you and God? If so, turn it loose and trust Him to give you the strength necessary to overcome it.

The love of ourselves is another garment we must cast aside if we would come to Christ. He said, "He that loseth his life for my sake, shall find it" (MATTHEW 10:39). As long as we are concerned only for ourselves and what we can get out of life, we can never possess Him who died that others might live. Consecration is the pathway to His power.

There are other hindrances in our progress toward Christ: the fear of what other people might think, the shrinking from the discipline of the Christian life, the fear that we could not live up to our Christian decision, the substitution of our gifts and services for the gift of ourselves, or it may be something else in our lives.

St. Paul went even further. Not only was he willing to give up that which hindered his spiritual progress, he even cast it aside if it hindered someone else. He said: "Wherefore, if meat causeth my brother to stumble, I will eat no flesh for evermore, that I cause not my brother to stumble" (CORINTHIANS 8:13). We must recognize the importance of our influence.

The thing to remember is that Christ is never willing to take second place with us. We must put Him first and desire Him to the extent that for Him we are willing to give up anything, even everything, or else we will never have Him.

The story of Bartimaeus ends: "And immediately he received his sight, and followed Jesus in the way." That is the final step. He got what he needed, he got off the sideline, he began to live again. It was a miracle, but one that Christ can repeat in the life of any person today.

In each one of us there is a mixture of the best and the worst. Each human heart is an unseen battlefield where the good and the bad are fighting it out; sometimes one wins and sometimes the other wins. When the bad wins out, we are ashamed and disgusted with ourselves. But when the good wins, we have a clean feeling inside and we are filled with joy; we have proven ourselves to be real men.

THE BEGINNING OF WISDOM

We are not wise enough to choose our own ways, so how can we know what God wants us to do? Proverbs tells us, "The fear of the Lord is the beginning of wisdom" (PROVERBS 9:10). Fear in that sense does not mean terror such as you would have if you were standing before some tyrant. The fear which is the beginning of wisdom is that which is born of awe, respect and reverence. When you see the majesty of the mountains and the greatness of the sea, you stand in awe of its Creator. When you observe the perfection of His laws and the righteousness of His character, your awe rises to respect. When you begin to understand something of His love, your respect rises to deep reverence.

And when one begins to reverence God it begins to show up in the way he lives. Dr. Sockman has said, "The man who does not reverently look up to something or someone higher than himself will let down to things lower than himself." But where is there one person who has lived a life good enough to stand before God on the Judgment Day? We have all sinned and come short of His glory. What then?

"For God so loved the world, that he gave his only begotten Son, that whosoever believeth on him should not perish, but have everlasting life" (JOHN 3:16). When we come to the final Judgment Day, our only hope is to come singing, "Just as I am, without one plea, But that Thy blood was shed for me."

WHAT IS HELL LIKE?

Hell is a place where there are no good things. There are no flowers there, no trees, no sunsets. Never is a kind word spoken there. There are no friendships there because there is no love there.

Nearly every town has a dumping place somewhere on its outskirts. Nobody wants to live close to the city dump. It is where the useless, unusable, no-account things are thrown. The trash of the city is put there to be burned.

Hell is the dumping ground of the universe. There is nobody there but those who are not fit for the city of God. The useless people, the "no-account" people, the trash of the universe. I think often of St. John being exiled on Patmos. There were many ways in which it was punishment to him, but I have an idea that the severest punishment of all was the people he had to associate with in that prison, where the worst of the empire were dumped.

Some people are so busy condemning sin that they have no time to do anything about it. Jesus was so busy saving the sinner that He had no time or reason to condemn.

THE OTHER SINNER

In a recent sermon I said the person who talks about one who sins is worse than the one who actually commits the sin. That is a rather extreme statement which I made extemporaneously in an off-guarded moment. I am not sure it is true. Yet I am not sure it isn't true. What do you think? Before you answer turn over and read the story about Noah getting drunk (GENESIS 9:20-27).

Noah was a preacher. Now, it is shameful for any person to get drunk, but for one who wears the royal purple of the prophet it is a double shame. Noah lay in his tent disgracefully naked. After a while his son Ham came and saw his father and he went out and told it. Noah's two other sons, Shem and Japheth, refused to look upon their father. Instead, they backed into the tent and covered their father with a garment.

Many generations later, when the author of Hebrews writes of the great men of faith, he tells of Noah's mighty work and does not remember his fall against him (HEBREWS 11:7). Undoubtedly God forgot it also. Japheth and Shem were blessed of God and they prospered. But Ham, the son who told of his father's nakedness, was cursed and was condemned to the life of a servant. Maybe, after all, he who actually commits the sin comes out better than he who tells about it.

Most things that are wrong are wrong because they knock us out of something better.

We cannot bury a live sin in a grave of forgetfulness.

PRAYER OF REPENTANCE

Time and again, I have prescribed to people the Fifty-first Psalm. It is David's prayer of repentance.

David had done wrong. He had reached the point where he could not continue to live with himself.

In that prayer he prays, "Have mercy upon me, O God." Justice is not enough. Only through God's mercy is forgiveness possible.

"I acknowledge my transgressions." He does not tell God he is no worse than somebody else. He pleads no mitigating circumstances. He frankly admits he has done wrong.

"Wash me, and I shall be whiter than snow." He has faith that forgiveness is possible. He believes that no person is hopeless in the hands of the Great Physician.

"Create within me a clean heart." He wants to be guilty no more. He is willing to change his way of living.

"Restore unto me the joy of thy salvation." He recognizes that happiness is possible only to one in a right relationship with God.

"Then will I teach transgressors thy ways." If he is healed he promises not to be ashamed of the Physician. He will tell others.

Those were the steps that David took after he had committed terrible sins, even murder. And they lead him to the place where, later, he could say, "The Lord is my shepherd; I shall not want."

It worked for David. I have seen those very same steps work wonders in the lives of many, many people.

A man is no stronger than his weakest moment, and every man has an Achilles' heel, a point of vulnerability. We cannot escape temptation because we are endowed with freedom of choice. And since no person has an iron will, everyone is in danger of falling. We can choose between good and evil, between being true and false, between being brave and cowardly, between being generous and selfish. And the very freedom of choice becomes in itself temptation.

WHEN EVIL IS CREATIVE

As you look back over your own life, ask yourself what experiences have blessed and taught you the most. What would you name first? Some picnic? Some light, carefree hour? No, you would list some sorrow or disappointment, some difficulty or frustrated hope, some dream that flickered and died, or some hurt that has left a permanent mark upon your heart. The most creative force in this world is evil.

Evil built our hospitals, our schools, our churches. The pain of sickness, the blight of ignorance and the burden of sin have been creative forces. Because of the pain of walking, we created a way to ride. Because of the suffering that a bitter cold winter can bring, we created a way to heat our houses. Nearly every good we have has come as the result of some evil.

And that is the way we want it. Lessing, the great philosopher, declared that if God came to him, offering in His right hand the whole truth, and in His left the search for truth and all the toil and pain and mistakes of the search, he would still choose the search. Not the finished article but the joy of a work to do was what he wanted. My little boy comes home from school to struggle with his home work. I could quickly and easily do it for him, but I would destroy his life if I did it.

We have all made mistakes. We get ourselves into situations which seem hopeless—some weakness in our lives seems as though it will ruin us—some wrong we have done weighs heavily on our conscience—some pain or physical handicap destroys the joy in living. We feel defeated and hopeless. Then we are reminded to turn to religious faith. Religion is betting our lives there is a God. Through our faith we begin to conquer the evil—our faith is the making of us.

HOW TO READ THE BIBLE

1. *Read uncritically.* As long as I live I will never forget the first time I saw my wife. I might have said to her, "The earring on your left ear is crooked." I say, I might have said that, but I didn't. The truth is I did not notice whether she had on earrings or not. I don't remember whether she was wearing a red dress or a blue one. I didn't see all those details. I just saw her.

I'll never forget seeing the ocean for the first time. I just stood and looked at as much of it as my eyes could take in. I didn't stop to analyze the water to see if it had the proper mixture of hydrogen and oxygen, or to see how much salt it contained. I just looked at the ocean and my heart was lifted up by the very greatness of what I saw.

Turn to St. Mark's Gospel and look at Jesus like that. Don't worry about every little detail; don't stop on some verse that is hard to understand. Read those sixteen short chapters as you would read any other story. Don't argue about Him or try to reason with Him. Just take a good long look at Him through the eyes of Mark. Get the full picture in your mind first.

2. *Read imaginatively.* Let your mind carry you back across the centuries and make you one of those who was actually present in the days of His life on earth. In the first chapter of Mark, you will meet John the Baptist—rough, fearless, truly great. Listen as his big voice booms out like the roar of a cannon: ". . . There cometh one mightier than I after me, the latchet of whose shoes I am not worthy to stoop down and unloose" (MARK 1:7). Does John sound as if he were talking about some pale-faced, anemic goody-goody who was weak and flabby? No. He was mightier than John. Let Mark draw the pictures for you, and one by one, let those pictures come into your view.

3. *Read devotionally.* You are not seeking information when you read the Bible. You are seeking to meet a person. Recall that in John's Gospel, Jesus is quoted as saying, ". . . he that hath seen me hath seen the Father . . ." (JOHN 14:9). Do you have questions about God? Someone has said, "I had a thousand questions until I met Him."

Suppose you were to sit down and write a description of the kind of God you wish we had. Describe His character and His activity just as you would like it to be. Then, as you read Mark's Gospel, you will find your own description expressed better than you did it yourself. Jesus was just what we want God to be. The best news ever given to man is that God is like Jesus. When the moment comes that you see God, it will be the most wonderful moment in your life. That is what we should get out of reading the Bible.

We must remember the difference in what God allows and what God intends. He allows sin. He does not intend sin. It has been well stated that "the capacity for sin and the capacity for communion with God are the same capacity." The freedom to choose evil and the freedom to choose God is the same freedom. For God to take all the evil out of the world would leave us spineless, jellyfish creatures. But to give us the power to overcome the evil through the cultivation of the good makes us like unto Him who is our God.

All men want to be happy, but we make a mistake when we think pleasure is the way to get happiness. There is forgetfulness of life's routines in pleasures, but they do not satisfy the soul. Pleasure is like dope; gradually we must increase the dose with more excitement, more thrill, more sensation, until, eventually, we find ourselves groping among the tombstones of our dead passions. It is like making our meals out of pickles and pepper. One of our greatest temptations is to put pleasure before God.

EMPTY HOUSES

One trouble with an empty house is it won't stay empty. You can clean it up, move everything out and lock the door but dust will gather in the corners, rats will gnaw their way in, spiders spin their webs, termites go to work on it. I read a lot of ghost stories, and usually the ghosts live in an empty house.

So it is with the house of life. Left empty, uninvited and undesirable tenants move in. In the first World War, the allied armies defeated the Kaiser but did nothing really constructive, and Hitler, who was worse, came in. The Pharisees in Jesus' day cast out the gross sins, but they developed no positive program and self-righteousness and hardness of their hearts took over. Moral reform is good as far as it goes. In fact, it is the first step to the possessing of the power of God. God cannot come into a life until we are willing to renounce our wrongs. But to stop there will result in failure.

There are many roads that lead to Christ. The Christian is not one who has gone all the way with Christ. None of us have. The Christian is one who has found the right road. Though you may not be at the end of your journey, if you are on the right road, at least your wandering has ceased. Even though you may not be home, if you know the way you are not lost.

9

Decisions Disciples Make

If we choose God, He must be the undisputed Master of our lives. The godly person is one who has no time of his own. He cannot say, "I will serve God during these hours; but, in my off hours, I will do as I please." There are no off hours in our service to God. We belong to him all of the time—while we are at work, at play, at home, and wherever we may be. The principle here is that one must make a definite and complete decision.

CALLED STRIKE

One of the great loves of my life is baseball. To be a great hitter in baseball one does not have to get a hit every time he goes to bat. In fact, a player can fail two out of every three times and still make any baseball team in America. But to me the most disappointing sight in a game is to see a player stand with his bat on his shoulder and let the third strike be called on him. To swing and miss is not so bad, but to stand there and not do anything is terrible.

So in life. Every decision one makes does not have to be the right one; even the wisest will make mistakes. But if you ever expect to succeed, you have got to be willing to make some decisions, to take some chances and go on. To stand through life with your bat on your shoulder is to fail in the worst way.

REMEMBER LOT'S WIFE

On one occasion, Jesus said, "Remember Lot's wife" (LUKE 17:32). She is a perfect example of indecision. Being the member of a family which gave us our greatest prophets and purest saints, there was within her the faith of her family. She knew God, and from her childhood had known the meaning of prayer. But, along with her husband, she had moved into Sodom, the city of mammon. More importantly, Sodom had moved into her: she wanted God, but she also wanted Sodom. Finally, the day of decision came. She made a start toward God, but she looked back toward Sodom. Reaching for the stars with one hand and fingering the mud with the other, she revealed her divided heart which brought misery and eventual destruction.

THE KNOCK AT OUR HEART'S DOOR

Jesus comes knocking at our heart's door in many ways. He knocks through our failures. Simon Peter, for example, never really opened his life to Christ until he had failed. He was too self-sufficient. But one morning, after a shameful failure, he heard the gentle knocking as Jesus quietly said, "Simon, Simon, lovest thou me?" (JOHN 21:15).

Sometimes we are so proud and pleased and filled with ourselves that we have no room for Him. Then perhaps our health fails, or we lose our possessions or job, or one of the children goes astray, or our home is broken up, and we are self-sufficient no longer. Then we might hear His knocking.

He knocks through our sorrows. Many people have told me that in the midst of a deep sorrow they felt the presence and power of God in a very special way. There is a little chorus that expresses it: "Just when I need Him most, Jesus is near to comfort and cheer."

He knocks through a vision of our better selves and our sense of inadequacy. We become disgusted and ashamed of the life we have been living. We come to realize we are made for a better way. But our efforts to change ourselves seem hopeless and futile. Then we hear His knock as He says, "Come ye after me and I will make you . . ." (MARK 1:17).

He knocks through the lives of others. When we come in contact with some person bigger and greater than ourselves we are inspired and strengthened. It may be the gentle goodness of a mother or the manhood of a father. It may be some person we know or a great life of history.

When God becomes the very center of our affection, our feeling, and our thinking, we shall find and possess and be possessed by God.

HOW TO MAKE A DECISION

As a minister it has been my privilege to talk with many people who need help on some decision. I suggest four steps that will do the job. The first one I got from Robinson Crusoe. Whenever he had an important decision to make, he would write down two columns of reasons, one for and one against a certain course of action. Then, with the reasons on each side lined up like soldiers, he let them fight it out, the stronger side winning. In any decision, the first step is to look at the reasons on each side.

The second step comes from St. Paul, "Let this mind be in you, which was also in Christ Jesus" (PHILIPPIANS 2:5). That is, imagine yourself thinking with the mind of Christ. How would He decide, if He were in your place? This step assures you of wanting to make the right decision, no matter what it might cost. Above all, we know He would do the will of God.

The third step comes from David, "He leadeth me" (PSALM 23:2). Keep saying those words until you definitely believe in the guidance of God. Mr. J. L. Kraft said, "I pray hard and think hard and when the time is up and I must have the answer, and I have done all the praying and thinking I can do, I just say, 'Lord, please show me the next thing to do.' Then, I believe that the first idea that comes into my mind is the answer. And I have been correct a large enough percentage of the time to convince me the process is sound." When you really believe in the guidance of God, then you will accept it when it comes.

The final step comes from Christ, "No man, having put his hand to the plow, and looking back, is fit for the kingdom of God" (LUKE 9:62). After you have made your decision, don't keep hashing over it. Trust your decision and go on, knowing God will see you through.

WHY I?

Someone has put the deepest question of mankind into just two little short words—"Why I?" In one form or another, that question has been in the minds of all of us. "Why I?" Until you ask and find the answer to that question, life can never mean its most to you.

"Why I?" I suppose there are some who never ask that question. Like hogs, they go wandering along through life with no goals or purposes, swallowing up whatever they can find that appeals to their appetites. That is the animal way of life. The higher human life searches for reasons to live. "Why I?" No more serious and important question can occupy your mind, and your real success in life is largely dependent upon your finding the answer to that question.

FOUR QUESTIONS

When I drive from my home to my office at the church, I usually come into Ponce de Leon Avenue at Ponce de Leon Place. I always seem to hit a red light there, and I do believe it is the slowest light to turn green in town. Then on down the hill at the ball park there is another slow light and then half a block on, still another. Then there is the one at Boulevard. I used to fuss about the delay of those four lights but now I have worked out a devotional period for them.

I have four questions I ask myself and take one at each light. First, "What am I most thankful for today?" Next, "What have I done during the past twenty-four hours of which I am ashamed?" I limit it to twenty-four hours because no traffic light is red long enough for any longer period. Usually I don't have the time to include everything even for the past day. I confess and ask God's forgiveness. At the third light I ask, "What is God's will for my life this one day?" Then at the last light I ask, "Whom should I pray for?" Every person can work out for himself moments of spiritual refreshment that make more real the presence of God.

No person ever really lives until he has found something worth dying for. You can never really possess the Kingdom of God until the cause of God becomes more important than your own life.

POSSESSING SPIRITUAL POWER

In the little city of Assisi, there lived a carefree youth by the name of Francis. He lived for pleasure and the satisfaction of his physical appetites. Francis was not satisfied with himself, but he seemed unable to change his ways.

One day he attended a little church. He came as most people come to church, not expecting anything to happen. The priest was reading some passage of the Scripture, when the miracle happened. The cold print of the Bible suddenly began to live for Francis. The life leaped from the printed page into his heart, and he became a transformed person. He began to preach with such winsome beauty and effectiveness that he transformed the life of his day. What happened? He became the possessor of a mighty spiritual power.

A story is told about an old preacher who visited Aldersgate Street Church in London. He knew it was the church where John Wesley had received that marvelous experience through which his heart had become "strangely warmed." He knew how Wesley had gone out from there, the possessor of a power so warm and yet so strong that through his preaching the moral tone of all England was changed and a worldwide revival was begun.

This devout old preacher asked the exact spot in the church where Wesley had been sitting when it happened. Reverently he sat down, lifted up his eyes and fervently prayed, "O Lord, do it again—do it again." And to this very hour, God is doing it again for those who really want to receive His power.

SOUL HUNGERS

We sometimes talk about the "free will" God has given us, as if He has completely cut us loose from Himself. We are not so free. We do not have free will when it comes to eating or not eating. Our very hunger demands that we eat. And God built into us certain other hungers. It is possible to live away from God and never hunger for material things. But there comes a time when those material things do not satisfy. We have deeper soul hungers and those hungers are cords by which God has bound our soul.

FREE TO CHOOSE

We were not free to choose the day and generation in which we would be born, our heredity, or even the color of our skin. Some are born with a talent to sing, others with a talent to work with their hands. But we are all free to use our opportunities or let them slip by, to double our talents or bury them in the weeds.

I am free to be good or bad, to fill my life with hate or with love, to live for self or to live for service, to make the world better or worse, to count for something or to count for nothing.

THE CHOICE WE HAVE

The laws of God are already established when we are born. His ways are fixed. We have a choice in that we can accept God's way and live according to His law, or we can rebel against Him. But we cannot change what He has done. For example, the world is round and the sky is blue. Suppose you don't like round worlds and blue skies. There is nothing you can do about it.

Also did God make the laws of the universe, which are just as unchangeable as is the universe itself. There are the seasons. The farmer learns the laws of the seasons and becomes governed by them. He plants his crop when it should be planted, and thus he reaps when he should be reaping. For him to rebel and plant out of season does not change the laws of God; it means only the failure of his crop. For the farmer meekness means planting when he should plant. It means submission to God's laws.

So with life. God has His will, and man has his will. Man has the choice of being meek or of being self-willed. He can say with Christ, "Nevertheless, not my will, but thine, be done" (LUKE 22:42), or man can say, "I will do as I please." The Psalmist says, "Delight thyself also in the Lord; and he shall give thee the desires of thine heart." (PSALM 37:4). On the other hand, to fail to become molded or controlled by God's will is to destroy ourselves.

THE INNER STRUGGLE

There are times when, with our limited vision, it seems that God's way is not the best way. We want material success on earth; we want happiness in our lives and peace in our hearts. If we believed, really believed, God would give us what we so much want; we would gladly be meek, that is, be willing to be molded and controlled by God. But it wasn't until he became an old man that Job knew without doubt that God is never defeated.

How wonderful it is to learn that lesson while there is still much of life to be lived. One of the sublimest statements outside the Bible comes from Dante, "In His will is our peace." The opposite of peace is conflict, and the reason we do not have peace of mind and soul is that we are at war within ourselves.

There is the voice of duty and there is the voice of inclination, both within us demanding to be heard. We struggle to decide, and the struggle squanders our powers. We become weakened and exhausted. But when one decides to do the will of God, day by day, as best he understands it, the conflict is resolved.

Such a decision takes all of the dread out of tomorrow. The wise man of the Bible tells us, "In all thy ways acknowledge him, and he shall direct thy paths" (PROVERBS 3:6). The very act of accepting the will of God for your life today places the responsibility of what happens tomorrow on God. So we do not worry about what the result will be. There is wonderful peace in leaving the results in His hands.

SQUANDERING OUR POWER.

I am sure that indecision is one, if not *the* most, harmful experience in the life of any person—harmful, first, because it squanders his energies. I still remember an experience that I had as a little boy. Several of us were playing in the pasture down by the side of the creek. We got to talking about whether or not any one of us could jump over the creek. I looked at the creek and said I believed I could do it. And the other boys dared me to try. I got back a distance, so as to get a good running start. As I was getting close to the creek, however, it looked wider and wider, and I began to have some doubt that I could do it. I started to jump at the same time I felt that I ought to have held back. The result was that I landed in the middle of the creek! I got all wet and was laughed at by my friends. If I had resolutely made up my mind to jump the creek, I believe I could have done it. My indecision squandered my power.

THE ROAD NOT TAKEN

One of the difficulties in living today is that we are burdened by our old decisions of yesterday. Where is there one among us who has not said, "If I had only made a different decision, my life would be better now"? Suppose you had married some other person, or entered some other line of work, or settled in some other city?

One help at this point is to remind yourself that you do not know the road you did not take. In your imagination you think of that other road as being smooth and straight and leading directly to your heart's desire, but you cannot be sure. That other road may have been more wearisome and more heartbreaking.

A second help is to remind yourself that you have not yet seen all of the road which you did choose. Maybe you are having hardships and difficulties now, but who knows—tomorrow may bring a turning point; if not tomorrow, maybe next week, or next month, or next year.

It is just possible that on the road you are now traveling, you will run head-on into happiness, the happiness you had begun to think was on the road you did not choose.

THREE WAYS OF SEEING

There are many things I would like to see—the Grand Canyon, some of the great cathedrals of Europe, the paths in the Holy Land along which the Saviour walked. I want to continue to see my home happy and peaceful, I want to see my children growing mentally and spiritually as well as physically, and some day become established in some useful work in the world. I want to see always the difference between right and wrong. Most of all, I want to see God.

But all people have not the same ability to see. Many people have limited vision. Some are cross-eyed. The eyes of some are weak and diseased. Some people have a growth called a cataract, which shuts off vision. Some are near-sighted, others, far-sighted; some are color-blind, others have blind spots in their eyes. Sidney Lanier looked at the muddy, crooked Chattahoochee River and saw in it a lovely poem; Joel Chandler Harris saw in rabbits, foxes, 'possums, and an old man named Uncle Remus, stories which will live forever. Woodrow Wilson could see a basis of lasting world peace, but tragically so few others saw it. Sir Christopher Wren could see a beautiful cathedral and make of that vision a temple to God.

There are at least three ways in which we see. St. Paul tells us that "eye hath not seen, nor ear heard, neither have entered into the heart of man, the things which God hath prepared for them that love him" (I CORINTHIANS 2:9). There we have pointed out three kinds of sight. There is the sight of the natural eye, with which we can see flowers and mountains, the printed words on this page, and people's faces. That is physical vision.

A teacher may explain to a boy a problem in mathematics or chemistry. As the teacher talks, the boy hears, and his mind takes hold of what he hears to the point of understanding. After he understands, he may say, "I see it." That is mental sight. In studying botany a student can reach the point of learning the various kinds of flowers and of their culture and development. Then he can see flowers with both his physical and mental eyes. If one understands what he reads, he sees with both his eyes and his mind.

But there is still a third sight, as when a truth has "entered into the heart of man." The heart has eyes, too. Wordsworth saw in flowers thoughts too deep for tears. Not only did he see flowers with his physical eyes, not only did he understand the growth and culture of flowers, also he felt their message. Jesus looked at people and had "compassion on them."

He saw them not only with His eyes and mind, but also with His heart. One can read the Twenty-third Psalm and understand the meaning of the words and phrases. But some read it and they feel the message and know the Good Shepherd. A boy can look at a girl and know that he loves her. He sees her not only with his eyes but also with his heart.

A person sees God through the eyes of the heart. "Blessed are the pure in heart: for they shall see God" (MATTHEW 5:8). Jesus said: "He that hath seen me hath seen the Father" (JOHN 14:9). Certainly not every person who saw Him with his physical eyes saw God. Mere physical sight of Him revealed only a man. It is not even enough to understand His teachings and His life. Many scholars have studied His words without seeing Him. Really to see God in Christ one must experience Him in the heart.

When the heart sees Christ, then we see God. To see God is to realize Him, to feel Him, to center the affections of the heart in Him.

Lesser people think about doing many things, but they concentrate on the difficulties instead of the possibilities until their chance is gone. Great men are not afraid to make mistakes. Great men are not afraid to fail. Great men have the courage to make up their minds and to act.

HOLY MATHEMATICS

Just suppose that there was only one real believer on earth and that during an entire year this one believer made one convert. Then there would be two. Suppose that during the next year these two made one convert apiece, then there would be four. Suppose that the next year these four made one convert apiece, then there would be eight. Suppose that they kept the pace of each winning one every year, how long would it take to convert every person in the entire world?

It has now been two thousand years since our Lord was on earth. Has that been enough time?Actually, there has been time enough, with just one winning one other per year, to convert sixty-five worlds like this. Starting with just one and doubling each year, at the end of just thirty-one years there would be 2,147,483,648 souls filled with God's righteousness. The next year they could convert another world the size of this one.

THE DIVINE TORMENTER

Jesus frequently is a tormenter of people. There are times when Christ comes as the comforter, other times as a disturber. Sometimes He brings peace, sometimes a sword. He may be a gentle breeze which soothes our wounded spirit, or He may be a violent storm which severely shakes us. We see Him weeping at the grave of a friend, and we also see Him with a whip in His hand, driving people before Him.

I have a friend whose broken arm had not been set straight. Not only was his arm crooked but it was also very painful. The specialist might have soothed and comforted him. Instead, he took an instrument and broke the arm again. That might have seemed cruel, but it was necessary in order to reset the arm straight.

And sometimes Christ upsets and disturbs us. He may throw us into circumstances which will change our way of living. It may be that just when it seems we have everything fixed, it all becomes unfixed. That business or friend on which we have come to lean so heavily may be taken away, and we become forced to learn again how to walk by ourselves.

Life itself is a disturbing influence. Styles change and we are forced to change with them. New knowledge is constantly being brought forth, and we must either keep up or be laid on the shelf. Living in a world like this it is impossible just to settle down. The procession will leave us behind.

The other night a man phoned me to say, "I am so miserable I can't stand it. I have done wrong and I must get it straightened out." Thank God that He disturbs us. If you feel agitated and disturbed, it may be because God is working with you.

The one thing we want is peace and contentment. But sometimes God will not let us be content in the state we are in. Because He wants the best for us, He will disturb and agitate us to keep us from being satisfied in some unsatisfactory life. Just as the physician may break a crooked bone in order to set it straight, God may break a wrong spirit in order to give us a chance to possess the right spirit.

By my bedside I keep an alarm clock. I don't like alarm clocks. There is no more distasteful sound to me than a clock alarming. It disturbs my sleep and though I dislike being disturbed, I set the clock. Why? Because each day I have new work to do. I have new opportunities to possess. And unless I am disturbed I will sleep my chances away.

Sometimes Christ is the divine alarmer. He disturbs our conscience because He has a better way for us to live. He makes us dissatisfied with the good because He wants us to have the best. He makes us ashamed of our ignorance because He wants us to learn. He shakes us out of our complacency because He has new mountains for us to climb which offer wider horizons.

Someone has well pointed out that God is one of three things to us. At first He is merely a void. Our belief in God is vague and unreal. But sometimes we are thrown into circumstances which our resources are insufficient to meet. We become forced to face God and often He then becomes our enemy. He makes demands which we find painful to meet. He demands new discipline and changes in our ways. We resent His interferences. But as we respond to God He becomes our friend. Void—enemy—friend. God is one of those three to us.

WITHERED HANDS

There is a story which begins: "And he entered again into the synagogue; and there was a man there which had a withered hand" (MARK 3:1). There was a man who was severely handicapped. He could think of a lot of things he wanted to do, but his hand was withered. He could not translate his thoughts into deeds. The hand represents action and his hand was withered.

In my work as a minister I have met a lot of people with this very handicap. They dream and they plan, but somehow they never quite have what it takes actually to carry out those dreams. A man was telling me recently that for years he has wanted to become active in the work of the church and make his life count for more. But somehow he has kept putting it off. He can't quite take the step. He has the right idea, but his hand is withered.

I have talked with many people who have a liquor problem. But I have never talked with any who weren't quick to say it was hurting their lives and they were going to give it up. But so often their hands are withered. They can't quite carry out their good thoughts. They lack the power to translate their desires into actions.

A man told me he was thinking of becoming a tither. I asked him how long he had been thinking about it and he said for several years. He wants to tithe but his hand is withered. He doesn't have the power actually to do what he really wants to do.

Look into your own mind and see how many good things you have there which you have thought about doing. But as yet you haven't had the right opportunity, or you lack the ability, or you don't have enough training, and haven't had time, or you don't feel like it—all those excuses are just other names for your handicap of a withered hand. You think well but you don't act.

To the man with the withered hand Jesus said, "Stand forth." That is, you have drifted long enough. Now let's face up to the situation. There comes a time when we must take command of our thoughts.

10

I Love Thy Kingdom, Lord

I believe in the Church prophetic, the Church that has a message of authority and that bows to no state or ruler; in the Church of worship, that instills the spirit of reverence in the hearts of men; in the Church of service; and in the Church that is to be, that will one day lift men above all divisions into one great fellowship of love.

GIVE YOURSELF AWAY

Jesus said, "Seek ye first the kingdom of God" (MATTHEW 6:33). In another place He put it this way: "He that findeth his life shall lose it: and he that loseth his life for my sake shall find it" (MATTHEW 10:39). The principle is clear: Get yourself off your hands by giving yourself to something greater and bigger. The greatest enterprise in which we can engage ourselves is to know God, to love Him, to seek to make God's Kingdom real in our own lives and in our world. Did not God create the universe, and does He not sustain it? Does not God cause the sun to rise in the morning, and the rain to fall upon the earth? Did not God establish the laws of nature and all of life? Has not God provided abundantly in every area in which man lives? "Wherefore, . . . shall he not much more clothe you, O ye of little faith ?" (MATTHEW 6:30).

Jesus is here laying down both a principle and a promise. The principle is: Fix your mind firmly on God; commit your life completely to His purposes. The promise is: All of the things that you need and really desire shall be provided for you. The Christian should reach the point St. Paul reached when he exclaimed, ". . . my God shall supply all your needs . . ." (PHILIPPIANS 4:19).

GOD'S LAW AND RULE

This world is God's kingdom. It is under His sovereign rule and power, controlled by laws. However, in foolish disobedience, man rushes on to destroy himself. Will we ever come to our senses? Will we ever recognize the law of God to the point of surrender and obedience to it? There are many who say no. They are so depraved, so corrupted by egoism and so blinded by pride that they cannot see the right way and have not the will to obey, even if they could.

Thus on every hand we hear destruction predicted for the world. We have eternal hell preached as our inescapable punishment. We are shouted at by would-be prophets who see no hope but only the terror of an angry God's judgment. But Jesus said pray, "Thy kingdom come." Surely He believed not only in its possibility but also in the actual event.

One night Jesus locked the door of His little carpenter's shop for the last time. He must be about His "Father's business." That business was to bring God's Kingdom on earth. The text of His very first sermon was, "The kingdom of heaven is at hand" (MATTHEW 4:17). That was the one theme of His preaching all the way. He never lost His faith, and even on the resurrection side of the grave He talked to His disciples of the kingdom of God (ACTS 1:3).

But we need to be reminded that in one sense God's Kingdom has already come. His laws govern the universe with absolute authority. The scientist knows the law of God. He sees it in the precision of the cosmos. The physician will tell you there are certain laws of health. To obey them is to have health—to disobey them is to die. The psychiatrist understands that a man's pattern of thinking must be along right lines. To turn off the track is to become unbalanced. Even the sociologist teaches us that the good of one is the good of all. We are bound together in a common brotherhood, which is a law of God.

God established His Kingdom on earth, which means His law and His rule. It is here right now. Whether we like it or not, His rule is upon us. As the prophet said in the long ago: "The soul that sinneth, it shall die" (EZEKIEL 18:4).

We see the capitol building of our state. We know the governor and members of the legislature. We think of how man makes his laws. Yet any and every law of my state can be repealed or amended. There will be other governors and legislators.

Not so with the laws of God. I could rebel against God's law of gravitation and step out the window of a high building. But I would only destroy myself. I would not change the law. So I go down on an elevator. Is that not overcoming God's law with man's mechanical genius? No Suppose the cable of the elevator breaks. It has happened. And the very fact that the elevator makers use such strong cables and regularly inspect them is a recognition of God's law and obedience to it.

Jesus had come to establish a Kingdom, but He was not a cheap politician willing to bribe people with a crust of bread. His Kingdom must be established by making men fit to live in it. He knew that mere outward prosperity without inward change would never be a permanent society.

The multitude always wants to make a king out of those who furnish easy bread. But Jesus came not to make life easy but to make men good.

THE GROWTH OF THE TINY SEED

Near where I live is a concrete sidewalk which is broken and ruined. In grading for that walk probably heavy and impressive machinery was used. The earth was leveled, the rocks were broken, and heavy concrete was poured. Unnoticed was a tiny sprout. Maybe it was just a seed. Surely it would amount to nothing crushed and buried under concrete. But that seed or sprout began to grow, and from the ground it lifted a section of that sidewalk until it broke open and set that growing plant free.

What a tiny little seed God planted at Bethlehem. Just a baby born of an obscure woman from Nazareth. Even as He grew He attracted very little attention for thirty years. As a young man He went around preaching about love and righteousness, about a Father and a new birth. In that day there were so many things so much more important to think about. They had to worry about the oppression of a dictator and high taxes, about building an army and the price of food, about business conditions, houses to live in, clothes to wear.

Finally He attracted enough attention to become a nuisance to a few leaders. They would put a stop to His silly talk. How? They would simply let the big and impressive machinery of the mighty Roman Empire bury Him. That was done. He was forgotten.

There were a few people, however, in whose mind that Jesus was planted. They kept talking about Him and for it they were persecuted, many were killed, but the ones left kept talking. Like the mustard seed, their movement grew. A tiny church was organized, then another and still another, until finally the power of the mighty Empire began to crack and it died. Not so with His church. It has grown to be the largest tree and is still growing. Jesus said it would happen that way. We can see He was right.

Just as men build telescopes to gain a clearer view of the stars, so almost since the dawn of civilization, have men built churches and set aside a day to worship, in order to gain a clearer view of God and the high purposes of life.

SILENT SERMONS

"Sermons in stones" is a phrase from Shakespeare. I think of that whenever I see a church building. We hear sermons preached in a church, but often the building itself is a more impressive sermon.

There is the *steeple* pointing into the sky to remind us to look up and think of God. As men go about their daily tasks, the steeple tells us not to forget those things which are high and holy. Atop many steeples there is a cross which causes us to remember Him who said, "And I, if I be lifted up from the earth, will draw all men unto me."

The *door* of the church represents the invitation of Christ, "Come unto me, all ye that labour and are heavy laden, and I will give you rest" (MATTHEW 11:28). Also the church door represents the Christ who said, "I am the door: by me if any man enter in, he shall be saved" (JOHN 10:9). The door should be open to all whose purpose in entering is to find Christ.

I think of the *vestibule* or foyer of the church as a place of preparation —a space separating the secular from the sacred. There one is usually greeted by an usher and given a program of the service. Also, it should be a place of prayer, preparing our minds for entering God's house.

The *sanctuary* is a large room designed to turn one's mind toward the Lord. As one enters he should feel, "The Lord is in his holy temple: let all the earth keep silence before him" (HABAKKUK 2:20). Even as Moses recognized that he was standing on holy ground at the place of the burning bush, so one should recognize the sacredness of the sanctuary.

High above is the *ceiling*. I like an arched ceiling that looks as though it were splitting the sky to let God and heavenly things come down. Also, as the ceiling is large enough to cover all, we are reminded of the sheltering arm of the Lord over all His children.

The *aisles* represent the opportunity of all to walk freely into the presence of God. The saint and the sinner each has the right of access to Him.

Within the church are the *pews*. They remind us of our promise, when we joined the church, to attend the services. Empty pews are a church's shame. In most churches the pews are long, unbroken seats upon which the people sit together as a symbol of the unity and fellowship of the church.

The *altar* of the church represents our prayers of adoration, praise and thanksgiving. The altar stands for repentance and forgiveness. It is the physical symbol of our own dedication to God and our purpose to walk with God in newness of life.

The *communion table* is where the bread and wine are placed, representing the broken body and shed blood of Christ. We sing a song which asks, "What can wash away our sins?" and then we answer, "Nothing but the blood of Jesus." His sacrifice is our only hope of salvation.

In the church are the *offering plates*. They are our invitation to share in the building of God's Kingdom. They are physical symbols of our inward dedication, reminding us of the solemn fact that "the tithe is the Lord's" and that we must not withhold from Him that which is rightfully His.

There is the *pulpit* upon which rests the Bible. From the pulpit are radiated messages of hope for the despondent, courage for the weak, comfort for the sorrowing, light for those who are in darkness, humility for the proud, and inspiration for all. The preacher is there to bring a message from God.

The *choir*, the *organ* and the *hymnbooks* remind us to sing unto the Lord.

THE STRENGTHENING FELLOWSHIP

Some people insist on going it alone. They do not make friends. They refuse to belong to a church. But there is creative power in fellowship, especially the fellowship of suffering. Even lepers found it so.

One of them had heard about Jesus. He told the others and little by little hope rose up in their hearts. They reached the point of believing. It is much easier to build up your faith with others than by yourself. That is why we have the organized church. The experience of the centuries has taught us that though people possibly can maintain their faith alone, it is much harder that way. Even in spite of leprosy, these men were determined to live.

There is a marvelous lesson here for those who are discouraged, for those who see no hope in the future, for those who would quit. Those people need the strengthening power of a fellowship. It may take time and effort, but it is worth it. I say to people who join a church, "It takes only a little time to put your name on the roll, but to become really a member of the church will take longer. It requires working with the people and becoming one of the many." Fellowship with others requires the giving of much, but eventually it means the getting of much.

CHURCH WORK

Ever so often some person says to me, "I want you to give me some church work to do." What he means is some job in the church—maybe playing the piano, or singing in the choir, helping in the kitchen, being an usher, doing part-time secretarial work, being made an officer of a Sunday school class, or being named to the official board of the church. All of these things are important in the life of the church, and must be done, but let us remember that these things are not really church work. The true work of the church is done through Christian lives revealing Christ in everyday work and play, and at home. The church work that counts for the most is being a Christian wherever we are, all of the time.

IS WORSHIP NECESSARY?

A lady told me she did not go to church because she worked hard all the week and she needed to rest on Sundays. That was her excuse. Her reason, not her excuse, was that she felt no need of God. Most church services do not begin until eleven o'clock. And then there is the service on Sunday night. She could at least get rested by Sunday night. She went to her work because she needed the salary she earned to buy food, clothes, shelter and the necessities of life. She does not regard the worship of God as one of life's necessities, and that is her reason for not going to God's house. That resting idea is no reason.

Many times the beauty of the Lord is expressed through formal and aesthetic worship services. But there is a danger of our services becoming so formal that they become dead. I have known people who go to a football or a baseball game, and in the moment of excitement stand on their seats and shout at the top of their lungs. Yet those same people would be deeply incensed at an outward expression of one's feeling in the worship of God. Frankly, I would rather try to restrain a fanatic than resurrect a corpse. I am not appealing for mere emotionalism in our faith, but I am appealing that the emotion not be eliminated. The Christian faith is not merely a matter of the mind; it certainly also is an experience of the heart and the feelings.

It is the Christian who can truly sing the popular song, "Don't Fence Me In." It is prejudice which builds social and racial and national fences. It is love that reaches out in compassionate understanding to all men everywhere. It is sympathy that bridges all the chasms that separate humanity. The Christian is so broad that he can carry upon his heart the weight of the world's hurt. The Christian is broad in that he gives himself to the building of the Kindom of God throughout the whole world, and there is nothing broader and more encompassing than that.

I was five years old when I went forward on the invitation to join the church. Some say that is too young. I can only answer it was not too young for me. Because I then wanted to live like Jesus as nearly as I could. According to some definitions of salvation, I was not saved, but if you consider one saved who is dedicated to the best he knows, then I was saved, and so is every other person who has made a like decision.

HERITAGE

As I stand in my pulpit each Sunday I am proud to be there. But as I look at the congregation I see men and women who have been there for forty, fifty, and even sixty years. For nearly a hundred years consecrated people have worked to build the church in which I preach. Back of that is upwards of two thousand years of Christian history, "in spite of dungeon, fire and sword." And still beyond are the prophets of old of Abraham's faith. All the chance and opportunity I have come from the contributions of others better than I. So nothing I could ever do would be equal to what has been done for me.

THE MINISTER'S LIGHT

When I started out in the ministry, I felt that the most important thing was preparing sermons. Sermons are important, but not most important. I was pastor of one church for twelve years, and during those years I preached more than a thousand sermons in that church. Were I to go back today and ask the people of that church, "Tell me the sermons that I preached here in this church," I daresay that many of them would be hardpressed to name even as few as ten of those sermons. But, on the other hand, all the people of that church would be able to tell me about how I lived, the spirit I had, the impression my life made. I now have come to realize that the minister brings the greatest light by the life he lives, rather than by the words he speaks. One is reminded of the old saying: "What you are speaks so loudly I cannot hear what you say."

The greatest temptation of religion is to become worship-centered instead of service-centered.

HOW TO WRITE A SERMON

Have you ever written a sermon? It is a very interesting experience. Every sermon ought to begin in prayer because the minister who does not talk with God in his study cannot talk for God in his pulpit. Through prayer one begins to feel the spirit of God and to understand the mind of God. Also, the minister must have in mind the people who are going to hear his sermon. He must love them and want his sermon to help them.

A sermon that doesn't help the hearer is not worth preaching.

With God and the people in his heart, the preacher is then ready to begin preparing his sermon. First, he needs a good foundation. Shakespeare said: "There are sermons in stones." But the best sermons are based on some passage of the Bible, which is the revealed truth of God. The purpose of the sermon is to make clear God's truth and then inspire the hearer to do something about it.

LESSON OF THE YEARS

I preach an average of more than 400 sermons a year. That is many more sermons than there are days in a year. It seems that the more one preaches the easier it would be, but, really, with every sermon it gets harder, and I will tell you why. When a young preacher starts out, he is anxious to impress people with his knowledge and abilities.

But as the years come along you get to know the needs of a lot of people. You soon become aware of your own weaknesses and inability to help, and you become less interested in trying to impress people with yourself and vastly more interested in trying to impress people with the One who can help. But He is so wonderful and your words are so weak that you close every sermon with disappointment in your heart.

AT THE ALTAR

Every Sunday night, as I see hundreds pray at the altar of the church, I know that some are finding God there. But long before time for the altar prayers I can almost pick out those who will be blessed that night.

Watch a congregation during the organ prelude and you will see a lot of difference. Some are quiet in thought and prayer. They seem hardly conscious of their immediate surroundings. Others are chatting away with everyone around. They watch others as they come in, note their clothes, and wonder about them.

When the hymn is announced, some sing not only with their voices but also with their hearts. Others just say the words or don't even bother to pick up the hymnbook. During the sermon some are like blotters. They soak up every thought and mood of the preacher. Others seem utterly unresponsive.

What makes the difference? Some have needs that human resources do not supply. They have come to church feeling that need, hungering and thirsting for God, and it is they who find Him. You never find God until He becomes your deepest desire.

11

Healing for the Troubled

There are vast numbers of people who are defeated in their lives. Their conqueror may be some wrong action, or it may be a mental evil, such as fear or worry. I am convinced that no person need be defeated by anything. Whatever the obstacle in the way of your success or happiness, on the authority of the wisest Man who ever lived, I declare you have within reach the power to live victoriously.

LIGHT AMID THE SHADOWS

Sometimes we are almost overwhelmed by the deep shadows which fall across our world and our lives. We become discouraged as we see the plagues of vice and crime over our world, the horror of war, discrimination against people, the low state of morals, and all the other shadows. But let us remember that shadows are created by light, and if there were no light, then there would be no shadows. The fact that we see shadows in our world is evidence of the existence of light, and thus the shadows become a source of encouragement and strength. The brighter the light, the deeper the shadows.

Put your hand in His hand, and God will give you the help to keep you brave as long as necessary.

All through the Bible we are promised dividends from troubles. Trials and tribulations are gold mines from which may be taken some of life's richest prizes. So, to begin with, instead of praying, "Lord, *when* am I going to get out of this?" it is better to pray, "Lord, *what* am I going to get out of this?"

THE WINDOW OF FAITH

In a church of which I was formerly pastor there was placed a series of twenty-three stained-glass windows depicting the life of our Lord. These windows were created by one of the oldest stained-glass companies in the world. For more than three hundred years this company has studied ways to create windows that will develop a mood of worship in the minds of the people.

The climactic scene of these windows is the one behind the pulpit, directly before the people during the service; it shows the ascension of Christ. More than half of the window is deep-blue sky. Some have said there was too much blue in it, but the artist knew what he was doing when he made it that way.

I was reading recently of a psychologist who had made a careful investigation of the effect of color on the human spirit. After a long series of experiments, he had learned that the color blue reduces tension, blood pressure, heart action, and relieves anxiety. Blue creates an atmosphere in which one can more easily throw off the worries of daily life and let the Spirit of God into his mind.

A friend of mine tells about talking with the man who repairs the windows in the Cathedral of Chartres in France. This man said that the one color which has not disintegrated under the elements during the centuries is the blue used by the ancient craftsmen. He declared that one reason Chartres is so stimulating to the human spirit is because of the deep blues through which the light filters.

The main point is this: if the color through which we look at the light influences our minds and spirits, how much greater are we influenced by the windows through which we look at life. Moses said, "Stand still, and see the salvation of the Lord. . . ." That is, first get God in your mind and then look at your problems through the window of your faith. Color your thinking with God and your anxieties will cease to dominate you.

GOD'S APPOINTMENT

It has been said that every man's life is a diary in which he means to write one story, and is forced to write another. That is, we plan for one way; we are forced to travel another. Here is a fine illustration of that fact: Writing to the church in Rome, St. Paul says, "Whensoever I take my journey into Spain, I will come to you . . ." (ROMANS 15:24).

To go to Spain was his dream and his plan. It was a thrilling and challenging adventure to which his soul responded. In his heart was the spirit of Kipling's explorer: "Something lost behind the Ranges. Lost and waiting for you. Go!" Instead of that great trip into Spain, he landed in a cold and dirty prison cell in Rome. Instead of the glory of conquest for Christ in faraway places, he was forced to face a prison wall and beyond that—execution and death.

Paul dreamed of going to Spain. Instead, he landed in a Roman prison, but instead of crying out against God or piously folding his hands and doing nothing, Paul dedicated himself, even in prison. Later he wrote: "But I would ye should understand, brethren, that the things which happened unto me have fallen out rather unto the furtherance of the gospel" (PHILIPPIANS 1:12).

Certainly every guard in the prison who came in contact with him was never quite the same again. If he could not preach to the multitudes in Spain, he would preach to the guards in prison. If he could not have the opportunities he wanted, he would take the opportunities he had. When you pick up your New Testament, notice how many of the books were written by Paul. Much of his best writing was done while in prison. There he found the quietness that he could not have found on his missionary journeys. I have no idea what victories he might have won in Spain, but I doubt if his contribution to the cause of Christ in Spain would have meant as much to the Christian world as have those letters he wrote while in prison. Paul's prison might have been God's will after all. His disappointment might have been God's appointment. Certainly Paul made it so, anyway.

But what shall we say of those crushing disappointments in life which do not turn into good fortune? Not every prison door opens out into centuries of service, not all valleys of the shadow of death lead to the brightness of the morning. Some of our disappointments we are forced to live with all the way.

When our little children go to bed, they do not mind having the light turned off, if the door is left open just a tiny bit. The realization that their mother or father is close by frees them from their fears. So with us. No matter how hard the struggle may be, how dark the future is, the realization of God's presence and power frees us from the bondage of fear.

Isn't it true that most of our worries are borrowed from some other day? We worry about mountains we will never have to climb, about streams we will never have to cross, about situations we will never have to meet.

Sometimes it takes a failure, or an accident, or some setback to make one think. Some people never look up until they are on their backs.

BREAKING THE FATIGUE BARRIER

William James spoke about "our first layer of fatigue." One may push and work to the point of exhaustion, and the great psychologist said that most people operate within the limits of this first fatigue; they never really accomplish much. He said that beyond this first level there is an inexhaustible power awaiting one who taps it.

Runners on a track team speak of catching their "second breath." Just as airplanes can break through the "sound barrier" so people can break through the "fatigue barrier." Many people go through life doing only those things they are compelled to do. For them life is a hard experience, and they are constantly tired. Others go beyond the call of duty and freely give themselves. They find life to be a stimulating, thrilling adventure.

All of life may be divided into two parts: the first mile of compulsion, and the second mile of consecration. In the first mile, one is constantly demanding his rights; on the second mile, one is looking for opportunities. The mile of compulsion is a burden; the mile of consecration is a great joy.

THE GIANTS WE FACE

David is not the last person to be confronted by a giant. In fact, we all have our giants, and that is why so many people develop inferiority complexes. If there were no giants, you would not feel inferior.

We remember how the children of Israel came to the border of their Promised Land. They appointed a committee to spy out the land. They found it to be a good land, "flowing with milk and honey," and they so much wanted to possess it. The majority reported, however, "there we saw giants, and we were in our own sight as grasshoppers" (NUMBERS 13:33).

Some of the giants in our lives are real. Others are imaginary. But whether they are real or not, the trouble comes when we allow the giants to make us as grasshoppers, "dismayed and afraid"; when, instead of giving our best, we give up and quit. Your giant may be some physical handicap; it may be a hard job that is before you; it may be a deep sorrow, a financial debt, a feeling of loneliness, a harmful habit, or one of many things. David did not minimize the strength of the giant, but neither did he let the giant minimize him.

SOME WHO FACED GIANTS

Whenever I get discouraged, I like to think about some of the great names in history and the giants they faced. Sir Walter Scott limped through life on club feet. Napoleon was an epileptic. John Milton, who wrote *Paradise Lost*, was blind, as was Homer, the great Greek poet.

Louisa May Alcott, who wrote *Little Women*, a book that has been read by millions, was told by an editor that she had no writing ability and advised her to stick to her sewing. When Walt Disney submitted his first drawings for publication, the editor told him he had no talent. The teachers of Thomas A. Edison said he was too stupid to learn. F. W. Woolworth built a great chain of stores, but when he was twenty-one years old he was not permitted to wait on the customers in the store where he worked. His employers said he did not have sense enough to meet the public. Josiah Wedgwood, whose name stands for lovely china, was a lame, uneducated, neglected boy. Beethoven was deaf. Before Admiral Richard E. Byrd flew over the North Pole and the South Pole, he was retired from the United States Navy as unfit for service.

Defeats can bless you because they make you more receptive to God.

The purpose of Christ was not to eliminate all the storms of life. He did not come to teach people how to have a good time and to avoid trouble. He came to create character. To His disciples He said, ". . . in the world ye shall have tribulation; but be of good cheer; I have overcome the world" (JOHN 16:33). And through His grace, we, too, can overcome our worlds.

THREE CHEERS

We talk so much about sacrifice, service, and the will of God that leads to a cross. We miss the truth that Christ's purpose is to make men happy; His typical greeting was: "Be of good cheer." In fact, it has been pointed out that He gave the world "three cheers." First, the cheer of forgiveness: He said, ". . .be of good cheer; thy sins be forgiven thee" (MATTHEW 9:2). Second, the cheer of companionship: He said, "Be of good cheer; it is I; be not afraid" (MATTHEW 14:27). Third, the cheer of victory: He said, "In the world ye shall have tribulation; but be of good cheer; I have overcome the world" (JOHN 16:33). What are the three things that destroy blessedness? A sense of guilt; a feeling of forsakenness; a fear of defeat. "Three cheers," said Christ; "I bring you the answer to all three."

Though God does not put a bed of roses on the battlefield nor a carpet on the race track; though He does not promise us an easy, effortless life, He does promise us strength and He does promise to go with us.

We should learn to stop keeping company with our failures. It is so easy to hold in our minds some miserable yesterday—to nurse it, nurture it and brood over it and eventually to surrender to it.

RICH DEPOSITS

I stood recently on a bridge over the great Mississippi river. I thought of William Alexander Percy's little book, *Lanterns on the Levy*, which tells about how the men would patrol the levies when the big river was at flood stage. The wives at night could look out and see the lanterns and feel safe, knowing they were being watched over.

Then I looked at that Mississippi delta land. And I thought of how time and again that land had been flooded and of how every flood was a disappointment to a lot of people. Houses were wrecked and crops were destroyed. But each flood left a deposit of soil, and today that land is one of the richest sections in all the world.

The flood of disappointment hurts, but it leaves life richer and better when it is rightly borne.

We believe God heals in two ways—through the science of medicine and surgery and through the science of faith and prayer. And those two ways are not in conflict with each other; they are wings of the same bird.

DIVINE HEALING AND DIVINE HEALERS

Some people feel one must choose between Divine healing and the healing through our physicians, hospitals and marvelous medicines. But there is no conflict between the science of medicine and surgery and the science of faith and prayer.

Luke was a physician when he became a Christian. He certainly believed in Divine healing and says more about it than any of the other Gospel writers. Yet he did not throw away his medicines after he became a Christian. He continued to practice the rest of his life.

A man suffering from diabetes came to see me some time ago. He said, "If I believed in healing through prayer and faith, does that mean I should not take insulin?" I said to him that God made insulin and that the physician is also a minister of God. And that God expects us to use the means at our disposal.

In fact, I refuse to pray for any who are sick who are not under the care of a physician. Our men of medicine and surgery, our nurses and our hospitals are doing the work of Christ, and to deny ourselves their ministry is to act very unwisely. I frequently tell people to go to their physician for diagnosis and such treatment as he prescribes.

The Christian ideal is a God-filled personality, not for health's sake, but for God's sake, and for the sake of our fellow men.

Even Christ could not heal the man against his will. To instill the desire for health in a sick person is often the first and hardest battle to win, and usually can be accomplished only by helping the person find a reason for living. If one feels strongly enough that he has something to live for, he usually subconsciously gains health-creating strength.

THOSE STILL WATERS

If you could look at this man who came to see me, you would think that he never had had a worry in his life. Big, strong, manly, successful in business, he owns a nice home, has a lovely family, and is highly respected by his friends. I was surprised when he told me he was sick and I suggested that he see his physician.

But he had already been, and, after a number of tests and examinations, his physician had told him he was in perfect physical health. But when he kept insisting that something was wrong with him, the physician had suggested that he have a talk with me.

I asked him his trouble; it was that he could not sleep at night. He told me he had not had a full night's sleep in six months.

I named a current book on how to sleep that is having a good sale; he had already read the book, and had not been helped. I asked about his bad habits, but he seemed to have a lot fewer than I have, so I dropped that approach. I asked about his conscience, but he assured me he had done nothing that was disturbing him.

I told him that he was not alone in his problems, that every night six and a half million Americans took a "sleeping tablet," but he said he had taken so many that even those did not help him any more.

I thought of giving him one of my sermons to read at night—I notice a good many people have gone to sleep while I was preaching them. I did suggest that he go to church every Sunday night—that will help a lot.

We continued talking, and finally he said, "I have everything a man should want in life, but I am just plain scared and I do not know why I am scared."

I took a sheet of paper and wrote across the top of it these words: "HE LEADETH ME BESIDE THE STILL WATERS." I handed him the sheet of paper and told him to put it in his pocket and before he went to bed that night to write down under the quotation everything he thought it meant and whatever related thoughts it brought to mind. Then he was to put the paper in his dresser drawer. The following night he was to take out what he had written, read it over, and add whatever additional thoughts had come to him. He was to keep that up every night for a week and then come back to see me.

I wanted to saturate his mind completely with that one thought. I know that it is utterly impossible to keep fear and thoughts of "still waters" in a mind at the same time. Any good fisherman can testify to that. That is the reason that fishing is such a great medicine for so many people.

There is no nerve medicine on this earth to be compared with still waters; when we create those clear, cool, still waters on the screen of our imagination, it is wonder-working. As Longfellow put it, "Sit in revery, and watch the changing color of the waves that break upon the idle seashore of the mind."

Well, I wish I could say that this man came back the next week refreshed, relaxed, and at perfect peace. But, to tell the truth, he did not come back at all. He felt he was too big and important for such a simple little exercise. He wanted me to tell him something complicated and mysterious, and when I told him such a seemingly simple thing to do, he was disappointed.

I would like to point out to him that greater scholars than he can ever be have studied that familiar phrase, and that no one has yet taken all the meaning out of it. And I would also like him to know that men become great because a great thought possesses their minds.

CONCENTRATE ON GOD

Hope is not a dreamy, unreal thing; it is based on the most real thing there is—the existence of the almighty, eternal God. The Psalmist said, "Why art thou cast down, O my soul? and why art thou disquieted in me? hope thou in God: for I shall yet praise him for the help of his countenance" (PSALM 42:5); that is to say, when you are disheartened, put God in the center of your thoughts. By concentrating on your troubles, you despair; by concentrating on God, you hope. If you will do that, the day will come when you will have reason to praise God.

When one stands at his full height in the face of obstacles, when one refuses to shrink back but instead gives his own best, when one sincerely says to life, "I come to you in the name of the Lord," the inhibitions are taken away, the tangles are cleared, and the clouds of life are lifted.

WHY CHRIST CAME

On my office wall hangs Borthwick's painting, "The Presence." It shows a beautiful cathedral into which a penitent, burdened soul has come. Her clothes are shabby and obviously life for her has been hard. But she kneels in the church and the presence of Christ is there by her side. As I look at that painting, I recall how one day He stood in the little church of His home town and announced; "He hath sent me to heal the broken-hearted" (LUKE 4:18). Not only do the wounded have the help of other people, they also have the help of God who is our Father.

COMPANIONSHIP PROMISED

Faith in God is not an insurance policy against physical pain; neither does it insure us against mental pain which results from such things as fear, anxiety, loneliness; neither does our faith protect us in every case from the remorse and agony over some sin of the past, though it may be repented of and now forgiven; and neither does faith protect us from the hurts and bruises which sometimes result from the environment in which we live.

> God hath not promised
> Sun without rain
> Joy without sorrow
> Peace without pain.

ANNIE JOHNSON FLINT

But God does promise His companionship, strength, and love. ". . .lo, I am with you alway . . ." (MATTHEW 28:20), said Jesus, not only to His first disciples, but to each one of us.

No emergency ever takes God by surprise.

In our desire for physical power, I am afraid many have lost inner spiritual power. The same God who created a power that can light up a room did not forget to create a power that can light up a life. The God who created a power that can pull a train across a mountain did not forget to create a power that can pull a person across the steep and hard places of life.

It is well to remember that if you never learn to let go, there will come a time when you cannot hang on.

Put a plank on the ground and no one of us would have difficulty in walking it. Lift the same plank high in the air and most of us would shrink from even trying to walk it. The plank is just as wide in the air as it is on the ground. The difference is that when it is in the air we think about falling rather than walking. And we usually do what we think about.

BLACKING OUT OR PULLING OUT

When you feel as the psalmist expressed, "Why art thou cast down, O my soul? And why art thou disquieted within me?" you can pull out of your periods of discouragement and depression. Down in Florida the other day a young man who flies jet planes told me their greatest danger in pulling out of a dive was blacking out. So it is in life. When our spirits are diving downward, it is easy to "black out" instead of "pull out." But you will never "black out" if you will emphasize these four things:

1. Never forget that you are important. No person created in the image of God is useless. Maybe you have not found the place in life that you want most, maybe your life doesn't seem big. But heaven has bestowed upon you a personality, one that no one else can duplicate. You were born for two worlds—this one and the one to come. You have been made

only "a little lower than the angels" and you have been "crowned . . . with glory and honour" (PSALM 8).

Because of who you are and what you are, you can afford to believe in yourself and depend on yourself. You are easily upset when you lean on other people, but when you have learned to balance yourself on your own feet, you develop a stimulating independence. If God had wanted you to imitate someone else, He would not have made you in the first place. Never let yourself forget that you are a person God made and wanted at this time.

2. In times when your soul is cast down, when you are discouraged, thinking all is lost, remember that you are needed. There is at least one important work to be done that will not be done unless you do it. We all give ourselves to something. Many people give themselves to something that is beneath them. Jesus said, " . . . ye are of more value than many sparrows" (MATTHEW 10:31), yet many people give themselves to nothing higher than what a sparrow gives himself to—just eating, sleeping, and the routines of daily life. In times of depression, think bigger thoughts of what your life can amount to.

3. When you get the blues, remember that there are several people in you. You are a good person, but you are also evil. You shrink back from life, but you also face a hard situation with calmness and courage. You have temptations to sink into some mudhole of living, but you also reach for the stars. Within you lives one who is careless and doesn't care, another who is greedy and selfish, another who is controlled by his passions, and many other selves. But never forget, within you there is always a best self.

You are the ruler over these various selves, just as a king is ruler over his kingdom. But sometimes we let one of these selves take charge of us and we lose control. The Bible says, ". . . he that ruleth his spirit [is better] than he that taketh a city" (PROVERBS 16:32). So when you are abnormally depressed and discouraged, it means you have let one of your inner selves gain control over you. You need to rise up and assert your authority. Never give up. You can always do something about yourself.

4. The psalmist tells how to pull out of those times when you feel depressed and discouraged. He says, "Hope thou in God" (PSALM 42:5). When you believe in God, you have hope; as the sun drives the clouds away, so hope chases away our blues.

One of the closest friends of Jesus was John the Baptist. They were cousins and probably played together as boys. One day the news came that John had been murdered. Surely it grieved the heart of the Lord and it was enough to discourage Him. What did He do? The Bible tells us " . . . he went up into a mountain apart to pray: and when the evening was come, he was there alone" (MATTHEW 14:23).

12

Look Forward Hopefully

> *There is a wonderful life within reach of every person—our promised land. God put it into our dreams; He gave us the ability to hope. But promised lands never come cheaply.*

ALL FOR THE BEST

Who is wise enough to plot his own future? We cannot understand a lot of things right here in the present. Why do we assume the enormous assumption that we have the wisdom to plot our future?

It is sometimes hard to see God's hand in some things that happen; you may not understand today why it happened that way. It may take a year or maybe even twenty years, but, if you keep your faith, eventually you will see that things do happen for the best. God will "give thee the desires of thine heart."

"Delight thyself also in the Lord." Don't get sour and bitter. Keep a smile on your face, keep "singing in the rain," and, above all, keep going. Remember, "He shall bring it to pass."

MAKING THE POSSIBLE REAL

Someone has pointed out that we live in two worlds—the world that is and the world we want it to be. Faith takes hold of the world that is, and makes it what we want it to be. Faith takes the possible and makes it real. It was the great William James who said, "As the essence of courage is to stake one's life on a possibility, so the essence of faith is to believe that the possibility exists." And believing that a better tomorrow is possible, we do have the courage to give our best to the creating of that tomorrow.

MEMO FOR THE DISCOURAGED

When you become discouraged, when life looks utterly dark, when your plans have failed, then you can take one of three ways out. First, there is the way of the fool. He says, "This is hopeless, so I'll quit it." "I don't like this job; I'll get another one." "This thrill has let me down; I'll get a new one." "My marriage is no fun any longer; I'll break it up." "I can't face this situation; I'll run away from it." The fool is always quitting. He never holds to hope.

A second way to face the troubles of life is the cynic's way. It is a little better than the fool's way but not much better. He believes everything turns out badly. "This is just my luck," he says. "There is no joy in life for me. I'll just bear it as best I can." He never expects much and thus he is never very disappointed.

A third way to face life is the way of hope. Of course there will be disappointments and setbacks, but hope sees the sunshine coming behind the storm. God gave us ears with which to hear because there is music to be heard. The Christian believes that. Also, he believes God gave us eyes because there is beauty to be seen. Also, he believes God gave us the ability to hope because there is something finer and better ahead and if we keep going, we shall find it.

The ability to think of the future is one of the greatest blessings God has given to man. If wisely used, this ability will cause us to plan and work for tomorrow. The realization that there will be a tomorrow is the basis of all hope. Man is the only creature on earth that can hope, because only men have the ability to think in terms of a tomorrow.

Every person is really two selves—the self he is and the self he has the possibility of becoming. Highest success will come to you when you begin to picture in your mind your best possible self.

THE TRACK OF LIFE

God cannot help us unless we are willing to cooperate. For example, here is a railroad track. The purpose of the track is to help the train get to its destination. But if the train decides it does not want to stay on the track, then the track cannot help.

God has said to us, "The track of life is my eternal laws. If you will follow it you can go a long way and life will be a happy and thrilling journey. But if you jump off the track, then you are likely to become mired in despair and frustration."

TAKING A LONG LOOK

Justice has a way of coming out on top. God so made the world to work that a man gets what is coming to him. A quick glance might leave us confused, but when we take a long look, we see that God causes righteousness to prevail. The Psalmist declares, "I believe that I shall see the goodness of the Lord in the land of the living!" And then he adds, "Wait for the Lord; be strong, and let your heart take courage . . ."(PSALM 27:13,14, RSV).

WILL POWER AND WON'T POWER

Within each of us there is both a will power and a won't power. We have high desires but at the same time we tell ourselves that it's no use to try. We say, "I will," but our minds shout back at us, "You can't—you won't." "Won't power" is simply will power in reverse. And it is easier for most of us to drift backward than to push forward.

HOW TO BE STRONG

One of the Ten Commandments forbids the taking of the name of the Lord in vain. We generally think of that in reference to profanity, but actually the most profane word a Christian can utter is "hopeless." The Psalmist repeats one question twice in the same Psalm; it is this: "Why are thou cast down, O my soul? and why art thou disquieted in me?"

Then, the Psalmist says, " . . . hope thou in God" (PSALM 42:5). The point is, when one believes in God, and has God in his life, he has strength and faith. The more reverent our attitude toward God, the stronger we are inside.

Hope is more than wishful thinking; it is a firm expectation based on certain fundamental truths and actions. Hope is never a substitute to clear thinking and hard work. On the contrary, hope leads one to think and to work. The foundation of hope is belief in God. The psalmist said " . . .hope thou in God. . . ." Read more of the sentence: "Why art thou cast down, O my soul? and why art thou disquieted in me? hope thou in God . . ." (PSALM 42:5).

The prayer of our Lord, "Nevertheless not my will, but thine, be done" (LUKE 22:42) is not insurance against some Calvary, but it is a guarantee of an Easter. That prayer is no protection against struggle and pain, but it is assurance of final triumph. Alexandre Dumas was right: "If the end be well, all is well." The assurance that the end will be well gives confidence to a struggling life.

GROWING GOD'S WAY

Some people seem to resent the fact that they are growing old. They hide their age in every possible way. Yet it would be a lot worse if, instead of older, we were steadily getting younger.

Just suppose the process were reversed. You would start living at an old age and every day be a little younger. Now that would be terrible. Every day you would know a little less than you knew the day before. You would start off with your grandchildren, but in a few years they would all be gone. Your family, instead of growing, would constantly be diminishing. You would eventually get to the age where you start to college. You would start off a senior and end up in the first grade. Now, little first graders are cute with their short pants or little pink dresses, but I would hate to think I would have to be one again.

Tottering old age has its drawbacks, but being a tiny baby is a lot worse. If you were getting younger, you would have to look forward to losing everything and end up by being a helpless baby with a bottle. Finally, you would just fade away into nothing. Babies do not have a previous existence, so complete oblivion would be the end.

No, I had rather grow older, gain by my experiences, keep up with the progress of this world, and look forward to a world where I will continue to live. The Lord knew what He was doing when He fixed things. He gave us the very best possible plan for life. Each day our life is richer. We know more, our experiences are wider, we have had chances to make more friends, we are more efficient and capable.

Something in man is always seeking a fuller life. Earth never completely satisfies him. Other creatures seem to fit into the world of nature, but the man is constantly looking for something else. I spend a lot of nights in hotels, but it isn't like being at home. And the Bible tells us that heaven is our home, the end of the journey.

SEEDS OF ETERNAL LIFE

Once they were building a new highway in England. It was to run between Holborn and the Strand. In the way stood a very, very old building. The workmen tore it down and cleared off the ground on which it stood. After the ground had been exposed to the sunshine and rain for some months, a wonderful thing happened. Flowers began to spring up, and botanists and naturalists from all over England came to study them. Many of the flowers were identified as plants the Romans had brought to England almost 2,000 years before. Some of the plants that sprang up are completely unknown today.

Hidden there in the ground, without air and light, the seeds seemed to have died. But they were not dead. As soon as the obstacles were cleared away, and the sunshine let in, they sprang into the fulness of their beauty.

So the seeds of eternal life are in every human life. But often those seeds are buried under such things as unbelief, selfishness, pride, lust, preoccupation, or some other sin. But when in humility and with child-like faith we bow before Him, it is the resurrection and the life for us. Marvelous things happen within our souls, and we become finer and better than ever we had dared to hope. Life takes on for us a new meaning, a new radiance and beauty, a new happiness, and peace becomes ours. We live again.

The rainbow means the storms are past; it is the symbol of hope beyond the tragedies. Here on earth we have troubles and heartaches, but there everything is all right. On earth man has done his worst; over there God has done His best—and nothing could be better than God's best. God is on the throne with a rainbow round about—nothing needs to be said beyond that.

CAME SUNDAY MORNING

What is it that takes the fear of death out of the mind of the Christian? It is Easter. Do not fail to hear the news as it is proclaimed. The same story is told over and over—it goes something like this:

A man by the name of Jesus once lived. One Friday He was crucified. After one of the soldiers had thrust a spear into His side to make sure He was dead, he probably turned away saying, "That one didn't take long." Simon Peter, one of Christ's followers, was heard to say, "I go a fishing." There was nothing else left to do. He had visions of Christ bringing in a Kingdom, but now He was dead. So it was back to the little boat with its patched sails, back to mending the nets.

Came Sunday morning. Three women had come to anoint His body. They found the stone rolled away and His tomb empty. Two of the women left. "But Mary stood without at the sepulchre weeping" (JOHN 20:11). She saw a man but did not recognize Him. Then He said, "Mary." The way He spoke her name! No one else had said it as He had. Just that one word, yet all of heaven was in it. She cried, "Master!" She knew. There was no doubt. It was He.

That afternoon some friends of His who lived in Emmaus recognized Him by the way He broke the bread. That same night, ten of the disciples were together when He appeared to them. They never doubted again. Eight days later, He invited Thomas to ". . .reach hither thy finger and behold my hands; and reach hither thy hand, and thrust it into my side:

and be not faithless, but believing." Thomas answered, "My Lord and my God" (JOHN 20:27,28).

Others saw Him, some through their physical eyes and others, like St. Paul, through the reality of a spiritual experience. They went everywhere telling about His resurrection. It wasn't a story they invented. Would any man have invented such a story in order to be crucified upside down, as was Peter? Or to get his head chopped off, as did Paul? Or to be stoned to death, as was Stephen?

The Bible says, "Then were the disciples glad, when they saw the Lord" (JOHN 20:20). The Greek word here for "see" does not mean to look through your physical eyes, as you look at a mountain, or at another person, or at the words on a printed page. The word "see" here means inner sight—perception—understanding.

"When the disciples saw!" They were never afraid again—not even of death. Peter was to be executed one morning at daybreak. The night before he did not pace the floor of his cell as some wild animal might have. Instead, he calmly lay down and went to sleep. When they observed the change in those who "saw," their enemies "marvelled; and they took knowledge of them, that they had been with Jesus" (ACTS 4:13).

We, too, stand before an open grave. We see One standing by. He calls our name. We can never explain it; we only know it is true. We "see" the Lord and we hear Him saying, "Because I live, ye shall live also." And we know it is true.

The Christian faith is never more triumphant than in the presence of death.

The assurance of eternity is our greatest incentive to a life of consecrated service.

UNLIMITED POSSIBILITIES

Man has an amazing capacity for growth. He only begins to touch his possibilities here on this earth. In heaven are lifted the limitations of the flesh and we reach our highest and best selves. We think in terms of little pleasures here. We satisfy ourselves with earthly joys. But when we become fully developed we will have capacities to enjoy so much that we cannot even conceive of now. So we are told, " . . . Eye hath not seen, nor ear heard, neither have entered into the heart of man, the things which God hath prepared for them that love him" (I CORINTHIANS 2:9). Jesus did not tell us more simply because we would not now understand or appreciate it. Sufficient is the fact that He is preparing for us—each one of us.

COME ON HOME

I used to play baseball, and my father went to the games because he was always interested in whatever his children did. I remember one game especially. It was a tight game, and I happened to get a long hit. I was running around the bases as fast as I could, but I seemed to gain added strength when I heard him shouting above the crowd, "Come on home, Charles, come on home." Since he has been gone, there have been times when the going was a little harder for me and I have been tempted to do less than my best, but then I could hear him saying, "Come on home, Charles, come on home."

Index

Accepting Ourselves, 66
Acquainted With God, 40
All for the Best, 181
At the Altar, 161

Bartimaeus and the Gospel, 124
Beginning of Wisdom, The, 127
Bible in Miniature, The, 102
Blacking Out or Pulling Out, 175
Blueprint for Believing, 96
Born Believing, 98
Breaking the Fatigue Barrier, 168
Burdens, 89

Called Strike, 137
Call of Love, The, 82
Came Sunday Morning, 186
Can We Know the Will of God, 44
Choice We Have, The, 142
Christ As Saviour, 124
Church Work, 158
Circles of Love, 79
Claiming the Power of Christ, 118
Come On Home, 188
Companionship Promised, 174
Concentrate On God, 173
Contagion of Christ's Love, The, 79
Convert Your Fears, 99
Courage Needed, 20

Developing a Christian Life, 56
Dialogue, 59
Divine Healing and Divine Healers, 171
Divine Provision, 110
Divine Tormenter, The, 147
Doctor's Prescription, The, 77
Dress Up a Life, 69

Empty Houses, 133
Equipped for Life, 60
Expressing the Experience, 86

Focal Window, 34
Foolishly Brave, 124
Four Attitudes, 76
Four Questions, 140
Free to Choose, 142
Friend of Sinners, 31

Giants We Face, The, 168
Give Yourself Away, 153
God-Given Faith, 99
God's Appointment, 166
God's Guidance, 48
God's Law and Rule, 153
God's Morning, 23
God's Plan for Your Life, 55
God's Purging, 18

Good Substitute, The, 66
Greatness of God, The, 39
Growing God's Way, 184
Growth of the Mustard Seed, 100
Growth of the Tiny Seed, The, 155

Heavenly Treasures, 90
Heights of Prayer, The, 133
Heritage, 159
Highest Room, The, 58
His Magic Power, 14
His Status Symbol, 21
Holy Mathematics, 146
Hour of Destiny, 86
How God Reveals Himself, 42
How to Be Strong, 183
How to Make a Decision, 138
How to Read the Bible, 131
How to Write a Sermon, 160

Image of God, 13
Ingredients of Prayer, 111
Inner Struggle, The, 143
Is Worship Necessary, 158
Is Your God Too Small, 101

Jesus' Formula for Living, 62
Jesus, Too, Had to Wait, 15

Keeping the Faith, 97
Key Ring of Prayer, 64
Knock at Our Hearts' Door, The, 138

Learning to Forgive, 84
Lesson on Forgiveness, A, 82
Lesson of the Years, 161
Life Is for Sharing, 73
Lifetime to Grow, A, 55
Light Amid the Shadows, 165
Live and Help Live, 89
Losing One's Life, 88

Magnificent People, 85
Making the Possible Real, 181
Meeting the Conditions, 111
Meet the Master, 11
Memo for the Discouraged, 181
Message from the Ocean, 62
Minister's Light, The, 160
Money and the Gospel, 90
Moving Mountains, 118

New Life, 49
No More Miracles, 32

Obedience Required, 33
Occasions for Prayer, 113
On Being Receptive, 107
Other Sinner, The, 129

Pictures for the Mind, 51
Positive Peace, 76
Possessing Spiritual Power, 140
Possibilities Come in Pairs, 67
Prayer of Repentance, 129
Prayer Suggestions, 115
Praying for Others, 114
Preparation for Prayer, 110
Principles of Happiness, 74
Priorities, 32
Profaning God's Name, 50
Proof of God's Love, 19

Remember Lot's Wife, 137
Rich Deposits, 170
Road Not Taken, The, 144

Seeds of Eternal Life, 185
Seeking the Source, 107
Seven Simple Steps, 108
Seven Words, The, 21
Silent Sermons, 156
Some Who Faced Giants, 169
Soul Hungers, 141

Squandering Our Power, 143
Strengthening Fellowship, The, 157

Take a Little Honey, 73
Taking a Long Look, 183
Testimony of His Critics, 29
Those Still Waters, 172
Three Cheers, 170
Threefold Confidence, A, 95
Three Prayer Words, 64
Three Ways of Seeing, 144
Track of Life, The, 182
Trust Your Heart, 81
Tugboat and the Dam, The, 61

Unanswered Prayers, 116
Unexplainable Mystery, An, 87
Unlimited Possibilities, 187
Unsatisfied Hungers, 41
Using the Faith We Have, 99

Walking With Christ, 17
Way of Christ, The, 14
What-Are-You-Going-to-Do
  Questions, 75
What Is Hell Like, 128
Whatsoever, 111
What the Creek Said, 63
When Evil Is Creative, 130
When God Says No, 117
When It's Dangerous to Pray, 117
Why Christ Came, 174
Why Christ Understands, 27
Why I, 139
Why Some Don't Pray, 117
Why They Sought Him, 27
Will Power and Won't Power, 183
Window of Faith, The, 165
Withered Hands, 148

Your Own Identity, 68